# SOCIALIST RAGS TO CAPITALIST RICHES

## DAVID G LLOYD

WESTBOW
PRESS®
A DIVISION OF THOMAS NELSON
& ZONDERVAN

WestBow Press books may be ordered through booksellers or by contacting:

WestBow Press
A Division of Thomas Nelson & Zondervan
1663 Liberty Drive
Bloomington, IN 47403
www.westbowpress.com
844-714-3454

ISBN: 978-1-6642-0178-1 (sc)
ISBN: 978-1-6642-0177-4 (hc)
ISBN: 978-1-6642-0179-8 (e)

Library of Congress Control Number: 2020915148

Print information available on the last page.

WestBow Press rev. date: 09/08/2020

# DEDICATION

This book is dedicated to my father, John Henry Lloyd, fondly remembered by many as Jack.

Real richness is when you are so expensive
that none can buy your character.

--Chaitra Gowda

# CONTENTS

# FOREWORD

The world is waiting, almost holding its breath for answers to hard questions concerning a frightening killer that has had it gripped in merciless hands. This evasive killer seems to be the personification of an evil that cannot even be seen by human eyes. Yet another deadly evil force that has chipped away at the foundations of our culture manifests itself once again in a back-to-back attempt at destroying our increasingly fragile and imbalanced existence. This time the killer bears the name of hatred working as a deadly epidemic of systemic racism that manifests itself as an obnoxious form of destruction woven into the very fabric of our national identity.

Strangely enough, neither form of evil nor hatred nor death nor destruction wears skin. None of them have a color or are exclusive to any one people group on the planet. These villains thrive on inclusiveness using hatred and privilege as platforms for spewing devastation on generations to come. We are all invited to play their pernicious games. David saw the same kind of privilege and destructive hatred growing up in the post-war UK. They seem to lie dormant in the heart and very nature of all mankind keeping us held hopelessly captive since we cannot eliminate or eradicate their ugly products that move like tentacles constantly grasping for victims among us, around us, within us. Even so, they have a common enemy in the form of hope and opportunity.

David was born in a particularly difficult time for England after the devastation of the second world war. Hope lingered in the distant future like the faint promise of spring in a wintry wind. Opportunity was even rarer, and survival more closely resembled the goal. He found that hope and opportunity were both the by-products of having a dream and holding on to it with rugged determination, sort of like the kind you need when facing a tough opponent on the rugby pitch.

The following story is David's acceptance of the challenge to seek a better way for himself. He met his challengers and some opponents by taking up the gauntlet of unknown adventure. As he grew to become a man dedicated to God's will for his life and the pursuit of a dream even though he faced powerful opposition from those who could not understand it, he persisted. He had the courage of his convictions that were desperately needed to stay in the race. David celebrated becoming an American citizen in 2014. As a citizen of both the United Kingdom and the United States, he takes great pride in both countries and wants to see them continue to do well and enjoy the benefits of prosperity and blessing.

He still finds valuable life lessons and unexpected challenges in the *land of opportunity*. The global pandemic followed by police violence and street riots reminded him to cling to a relationship with a known God through Jesus Christ. He learned that the equality of opportunity that he admired on this side of the Atlantic is, sadly, not always equal. But there is continual hope for the land of the free and the home of the brave.

David believes that the answers lie firmly in the hands and in the vast plan of God, the creator of all. His story is worth the read if you want to have a front-row seat to a captivating life in the second half of the twentieth century, a century not to be soon forgotten and one that has made such an enduring impact on the world that we know today.

# PREFACE

I recently heard American political pundits stating that the European examples of socialism work well. These statements frequently come from those who have not experienced the realities of living under this kind of theory. The pages that follow are my testimony and my first-hand knowledge that the "European Socialism" to which they refer does not work. In the years after the last World War, our lives were hard. There was little extra, so no extravagance whatsoever. There was not much fun to enjoy, and taxation seemed to go after even the tiniest of luxuries. There was never enough money for anyone or anything. Great Britain decided that the answer to multiple recovery problems was in socialistic ideology and austerity measures. It was the way to go. However, its proponents soon discovered the predicament of seemingly, insurmountable and constant problems that arose from the nationalization of companies like the Railway System, the National Health Service, the coal industry, and the steel industry. In the late seventies, both the government officials and the people grew more and more frustrated by the continual strikes that were crippling a country that was literally under the control of the unions and union leaders.

I am a happy, naturalized citizen of the United States. I also hold citizenship in the United Kingdom, my home country, and place of my birth after having maintained and cherished my love and deep connections there. I consider myself to be very fortunate, indeed, to have been born and raised in Great Britain and also to have had the privilege of realizing my life dream of being a part of what I believe is the greatest nation in the world even with her imperfections. I have years of experience developing my businesses in the United Kingdom. I have also been blessed to enjoy setting up and benefiting from my American business ventures. The excitement for me has been in finding that there were really few limitations for my ideas and experience as long as I diligently sought the right locations and avenues and I was willing to put in the work and determination needed to build my business.

Warrington, where I was born and raised, was also a town that was among the most socialistic in England. Its citizens continue today to vote overwhelmingly for the particularly socialistic and very left-leaning Labour party in every election.

After the 2010 national elections, and a conservative victory, Liam Byrne, who was former Treasury Chief Secretary from the Labour party, left a handwritten note in the Treasury office. The note was only 16 words in length. It offered no explanation, apology, or justification for the nation's dismal financial condition that the new government was inheriting.

*"Dear Chief Secretary, I am afraid there is no money. Kind Regards and Good Luck, Liam"*[1]

His pleasant, little note caused considerable problems for the modern Labour party.

After growing up in the northwest sector of the United Kingdom, I have what I consider to be extensive first-hand experience about the hidden dangers and notable problems of socialism for a people group who find they are either moving willingly or unwillingly towards a socialistic regime. The sharing of my story should bring a foreboding word of caution and a chilling wind to those currently considering these extensive socialistic changes to the American way of life.

# ACKNOWLEDGMENTS

This story would not have unfolded, nor would the book have been written without the inspiration and support of God's constant hand in my life. My upbringing from being a little lad through all the days of my life portrays His love and His unbelievable creative design. I am thankful beyond my ability to describe.

My parents, my first wife, Barbara, who is now in heaven, my three sons, Simon, Philip, and Ben along with my daughters-in-law, my grandchildren, my family, and friends on both sides of the Atlantic Ocean are all amazing people. They have been a tremendous blessing and a source of more enthusiastic encouragement than any one person could expect during any one lifetime. I am humbled by and grateful for the love and beauty they constantly show me.

I want to thank my dear friends, San Ireland, and Dr. Sandy Gruskin, who gave valuable suggestions and corrections for this project. Much gratitude goes to my son, Ben, for his beautiful photos included in the book and to my brother-in-law, Ray Gambrell, for the stunning cover photo.

Finally, I am indebted to my wife, Lynette, who provided her assistance and contributed long work hours dedicated to me in the writing of this book. She caught the vision of the importance of my story in its early stages. We believed, together, in the impact that the telling of our story might have on the rapidly changing landscape of our world during these beginning years of the second millennium.

*One*

# FATHER KNOWS BEST

Of all the titles I've been privileged to have,
"Dad" has always been the best.

-Ken Norton

My father, John Henry Lloyd was born in 1916 right in the middle of World War I. He was the eldest of six siblings. The family lived in the northwestern town of Warrington in Cheshire. Poverty was a problem for many in Great Britain in the early half of the twentieth century and the devastating world wars made things even more difficult for both the country and people.

When Jack came of age, he married my mother, Charlotte. I was the youngest of three children. Jack tried to teach us to be virtuous and respectful of the teachings of the Holy Bible. Our family spent much time in church especially since my dad was a lay preacher. It has been said before that the preacher's kids can sometimes be the hardest to teach. Jack managed to get his message across to us kids, but it was not always a smooth process.

I am grateful that my father taught me to know myself, to work hard, to care for those who looked to me for support, and to recognize the often hidden dangers of false doctrines and rhetoric that negatively impact our culture in the name of progress. As we listened to the speeches of certain politicians advocating passionately for socialistic ideologies when I was a boy, even though there were many in our town struggling to provide for their families, my dad used to comment about their socialistic goals. "My, my, what a load of complete and utter nonsense!" My first reaction to my strong-minded father's opinion, since I was a youngster who thought he knew more than his old man, was laughter and skepticism at his words. However, after years spent living in England's socialistic north, I realized the accuracy of my father's observations.

Jack grew up in England during two world wars. The nation was greatly impacted by both of them. He served in World War II and was stationed in India. He knew well what poverty looked like. As a young boy, he and his younger brother Joe wagged school (for those of you who do not know English speak, that means they played hooky as often as possible). Of course, they were caught but education was not a top priority or even an important part of life.

Jack had a strength of character and strong convictions that stemmed from his firm foundation of faith. He was a natural leader since he was the eldest of six children.

My father was a man who avidly devoured the holy scriptures. It was a pleasure for many to talk about them with him and learn from his knowledge. He is well remembered for many delightful moments but certainly for his sharp expertise. Whenever you wanted to know where something was in the Bible, you only had to ask. He would answer, "Give me a moment." Then he would tell you exactly where to find what you were searching. Even at ninety-two years old, he had no trouble remembering a scripture or even a phone number. And of course, he could talk forever about the implications of God's truths and what they mean for us. He could out remember the lot of us! It was quite impressive!

He was a fair-minded man with a deep respect for the human experience. He was respectful of all people throughout the whole world. He was born in Warrington, known then as Lancashire in the United Kingdom. Warrington is now a part of Cheshire as a result of local government reforms. Jack served in World War II in the Royal Corp of Signals Brigade. His job was to repair wires to keep the crucial lines of communication open. He was stationed in France and India and spent four years away from our family. He remembered a large number of losses of life from battle and told us about the large numbers of corpses he saw while serving the country.

Once on a visit to the state of Georgia, while walking the grounds of Stone Mountain, we encountered the war memorial of the Confederate generals. On the ground was a memorial plaque stating that the monument was a reminder of "a revered way of life." My dad commented that this was indeed a matter of opinion. Not everyone could possibly agree since there had been a civil war in the United States over the "way of life" problem.

Since I was raised in a strict Christian home, as a young man I sometimes questioned the value of being the child of a lay preacher. Dad preached at different churches throughout the north of England. My siblings and I were taught all the important rules and precepts of the Bible, which at the time I failed to fully appreciate. I was the proverbial son who thought he knew more than his old man. I have learned throughout the years that my parents were wiser than I wanted to acknowledge. But I became living proof for the directive that says to train a child in the way that he should go and when he is old, he will not depart from it.

My father's background, his education, self-instruction, and his victimization by the wheels of the socialistic welfare state hindered this intelligent, self-motivated, and self-educated man. Jack had admirable and sometimes annoyingly strong values (at least they were annoying to me since I was also a mischievous boy), and he did not mind telling them to you one bit. Yet because he was born into poverty that prevented him from benefiting from a good educational foundation and from having a reasonable opportunity to make an impact on his generation, he became a victim of the socialistic ideology of his time. Poor education, welfare state provisions, and austerity measures for the country, in general, provided relatively few good opportunities for career development unless your family was wealthy. The social hierarchy was well in place by the time he began to pursue a living and to care for his family. Jack learned to make do with what he had along with just about everybody else in the northwest of Great Britain. Making do was the name of the game.

Middle left forefront, Jack Lloyd on Walking
Day, Warrington in the mid 50's

*Two*

# GROWING UP IN THE NORTHWEST OF ENGLAND

And did those feet in ancient time
Walk upon England's mountains green
And was the Holy Lamb of God
On England's pastures seen!

Jerusalem (And did those feet in ancient time)

--William Blake 1804

I was born in Warrington during the summer of 1949, the period of recovery in the United Kingdom after the devastations of World War II. I grew up in the industrial town of Warrington, located in the northwest of England. Even though my hometown was considered an industrial one in the north, the surrounding countryside was quite beautiful.

The Romans founded Warrington at a location convenient for crossing the River Mersey. Later a new settlement was established there by the Saxons, which means that the history of the people now living in the area developed under the influence of immensely powerful tribes and warriors from Germanic, Viking, and Roman ancestry. The people of the North of

England descended from potent stock. It is not surprising that even today, there are "tribes" that regularly clash on the soccer and rugby pitches since tribal wars are no longer encouraged. Today they are called matches and are eagerly attended and followed by the locals.

In the Cheshire area where Warrington is situated, there are numerous monuments, several old churches from centuries past, famous rivers, and historical sites. In and around Cheshire, you will find Roman gardens, settlement walls, and amphitheaters dating from as far back as seventy AD. You will also find Tudor heritage-listed buildings from the sixteenth century, country estates from England's past landed gentry, and even what was probably the remains of a relic from the Bronze Age that we called Jacob's well. The well is in a natural wall embankment dating back much further than anyone could ever recall. It is possible that the relic dates back as far as 1900 BC since that is the time that people began to use bronze for tools and weapons in England.

There is a large, beautiful, well-maintained garden at the Walton Estate dating from the 1830s that has been opened to and maintained by the public since 1941. Even now, there is an elaborate system of several beautiful gardens and greenhouses where one can stroll for hours. We recently hosted and toured some of the well-known, historical sites of Great Britain with close American friends on a hike through the town and country. We spent precious moments strolling through Walton Park on one of those rare, sunny days last autumn. They were able to identify many varieties of trees, shrubs, and flowers.

It was great to be able was to show them my old stomping grounds from what seemed to be ages ago. It was here that we played as children so many years ago and then, in turn, took our own children to play, watching them for endless hours on the few sunny days that characterized the short but wonderful English summer.

Not long ago it seems, we took one of the grandchildren on a play day in Walton Park when she was about six years old. We often enjoy taking the grandchildren out on adventures. There are seven of them and we have had lots of memorable laughs and adventures. It is only by God's grace and blessing that I have been so fortunate.

That day at the park, the little one ran so fast through the park along the paths, rounding corners so fast that we could barely keep up with her. What if someone had grabbed her? We were scared silly that she would get into serious trouble. Of course, that would have been the end of any play days ever again permitted by the parents.

This one was probably paying us back for all the trouble that I caused my parents when I was about that age. That little one has grown into a beautiful, young woman just like her cousins. When I honestly admit how fast life goes, I realize that it must be a little longer back than I want to admit. These lovely, young ladies are all beautiful, English roses and I am proud to be the grandfather of them all. Sometimes I find it hard to believe that they came from my stock and from my heart, that same rugged, northern warrior stock that marked my ancestors and the people of Warrington. But then again, not one of them is a pushover. They have all done justice to their ancestry.

There was a canal running through Walton Park that we used for fishing and swimming when we could manage to get away with it. Since swimming was not officially allowed in the Bridgewater Canal, it was certainly another way to get into mischief. It seemed to be just what you did as a kid. We had loads of fun getting into trouble. There were not so many restrictions for children in the somewhat smaller and relatively safe community where we lived. There were plenty of places that my friends and I could get into trouble while our parents were all working hard. There were lots of laughs, but also some yelling and spanking. Even though he was strict, my dad was a softie and would come to tears sometimes after giving us a "good hiding" as he used to call it. His words were, "do as you're told, or I will give you a jolly good hiding." He would then apologize after the hiding probably remembering that he was just the same kind of kid.

Charlotte, David, and cousins

My mother was named Charlotte, but everyone called her Lottie since we always break down names in this part of the country. She was a dark-haired English beauty with a melodious singing voice and a strong personality. She knew what she wanted and was certainly not a shrinking violet. My mum often sang solos at the church.

She decided one day that she wanted to open her own confectioner's shop and proceeded to secure a loan from the bank without even telling my father. He laughed about it all but was quite proud of her. Soon, Lottie had a busy and thriving bakery business. She made the most delicious and sugary, mouth-watering pastries. Everyone in the neighborhood wanted to indulge themselves with a little something sweet and wickedly delightful. I can trace my entrepreneurial spirit right back to my mother. Of course, as a young lad, the shop was one of my favorite places to be since I got to taste more than my share of goodies and developed a voracious sweet tooth. But I carefully watched her as she worked hard and for long hours.

Fortunately, during those days, our home was just steps away above the shop. She was up at four am to bake the bread and stayed in the shop below until 8 pm just about every night. Then she took good care of the entire family, making sure that we were well fed and off to bed. I learned a lot from her innate business sense. I learned how to care for the people who work for you and how to treat them like valued members of your family while still making a good profit.

Gwen, David, and Alan

Close friends of my parents who were dairy farmers lived in Nantwich, a historical township not far from Warrington. Nantwich, occupied by the Romans and the Normans, was mentioned in the Doomsday Book of 1086. The town is known for its delicious cheeses, delightful open countryside, stunning gardens, and elegant ancient buildings some of them tracing their inspiration to donations from Queen Elizabeth I in the 1500s after a fire nearly devastated the town. It is located about 30 miles away from Warrington in the historical area of Chester. I spent several memorable weekends visiting the farm and helping with the chores. I loved the smells, the haymaking, riding horses and, milking the cows. I will probably never forget the smell of hay and horses. Whenever I am fortunate enough to be out in the open countryside near farms or when I see hay harvested, I am transported right back to those idyllic days.

One of my most enjoyable memories of school days was when I got the chance to ride horses at the Stretton Stables. I would ride them back to the stables in the evening for the owner. Once while heading to the stables, I was riding a large, white cob horse named Nora. A local police officer stopped me since I had no lights on the horse. I had never heard of that happening to anyone before or since. Even though I was on the footpath and the horse was unmistakably white, and not to be missed, the officer was adamant. Fortunately for me, he could also see my dilemma and allowed me to continue the last mile to the stables.

English countryside

The English countryside still has not changed that much. It is still incredibly beautiful, and it will always remain a part of the unforgettable memories of my life story. From the age of eleven through thirteen, I worked my summer holidays on a local farm in Whitley, another small town near Warrington. I loved the farm so much that I wanted to be a caretaker farm manager, but life would take me in a different direction.

I found time to be a part of the St Thomas' Anglican Church Boys Choir in Stockton-Heath. My mother was a talented singer, and as a young lad, I also loved to sing and make as much music or noise as they would allow me to make. Because of a fair amount of talent on my part and a good boy soprano voice, I won the opportunity to sing in the county Choir of Cheshire when I was fourteen. It was quite an honor, but I started working at a job as an apprentice engineer at fifteen. The conflict of schedules prevented me from continuing with my choir responsibilities. Looking back, I wish that I had taken the somewhat prestigious opportunity, but how could I have possibly convinced my fourteen-year-old self that this kind of prestige would ever be important to my life.

Warrington Parish Church
courtesy of Benjamin D. Lloyd

Saint Thomas Church of Stockton Heath
courtesy of Benjamin D. Lloyd

My extra-curricular activities as a young student, apart from sport would have to wait. Talent would have to take a back seat. It would be another thirty-six years or so before I would be able to get back into a choir even if only for fun.

For most of my peers, the task of getting a job and becoming a wage earner was considered the most important goal in life rather than the development of artistic potential. There was never a discussion about career choices for most of us. There were not abundant choices for extracurricular activities since life was more about finding work and getting a job. The system of the welfare state was not geared to helping young people develop careers that would provide a good living for their futures. The state system was directed to produce workers and was still in the same stages as they had been during the Industrial Revolution. School was not a place to develop ambition. The question of what you would like to be when you grew up was rarely discussed. We were following the same working-class track that our parents had laid out before us, and before that, their parents had laid out the same option available for them. Your only choice was that you would probably work for someone else. There were plenty of industrial jobs available and plenty of companies that needed workers in Warrington. It was not surprising for us since school did not seem at all to be a place that would prepare you for a professional career. On looking back, our educations seemed more like indoctrination intent on leading us to accept our futures as workers not helping us to develop our talents and abilities to have meaningful lives.

There are disturbing similarities in the American public-school education system as we often see a failure to adequately prepare children for taking successful and productive places in a competitive world market and economy. The idea of "free stuff" and substantial care from the government is becoming a by-product of getting an American education. After spending several years as a teacher at the university and elementary level, my wife has experienced conditions, especially in the elementary schools, that sadly resembled babysitting assignments. There were inadequate resources, unethical usage of critical administrative funding in some school districts, and sometimes poorly trained educators doing the best that they could while working under harsh conditions at all levels of these systems. Teachers, for the most part, are frustrated, often overworked and always underpaid with large numbers of students in crowded classrooms coming from various backgrounds, cultures, and levels of the lower socio-economic landscape crowded into the one size fits all classroom scenario.

At the university levels, most public university students are not being or have not been taught or encouraged to think for themselves to make rational decisions. These students are more prone to being spoon-fed the philosophies and mentalities of their left-leaning professors. At the same time, tuition and fees continue to spiral upwards in such a way that causes most college-educated graduates to incur massive debt burdens from student loans before they can even obtain their first employment. Strangely enough, this system resembles a perfect model of the brink of disaster socialistic problem like the educational system in which I was enrolled as a youngster because there was just never enough of what was needed for individual success. Since our children are the future, these present conditions should serve as an ominous warning. I have heard that children are the messages we leave for the future. What exactly are we saying to those who will look back?

As I grew older, I developed a passion for Rugby League. Warrington was a Rugby League town and I have always been an avid supporter. Even today, when I visit, I try to fit in a match as often as we can. Competitive sports events and competition in general is in my blood since my father was also

13

an avid cricket fan and a big Everton Soccer fan. A passion for competitive exchange goes back quite far in my ancestry since we originate from this part of the United Kingdom for as far back as can be remembered. We are all passionate Manchester United supporters and enjoy watching and playing all sport such as American football even though it is vastly different from what we call football on this side of the Atlantic. For me, there are few things more stimulating than enjoying an afternoon at Old Trafford "the Theater of Dreams" or Rugby League match at Halliwell-Jones Stadium in Warrington with my sons. On a recent birthday that I was celebrating with them all, they treated me to an excellent game and delicious meal.

Since primary school and up until the age of thirty-three, I played the popular, fast-paced, rigorous, contact sport of Rugby League with determined energy and a concentrated effort. That effort was always enthusiastically matched by my rugby mates. Yes, a competition that required your best effort on the pitch was ingrained in me probably much further back than I even know. It's not surprising that I would choose a competitive free market economy over a state-run welfare system.

I spent part of my early school years in Stockton-Heath, a small, village community located just minutes away from where I would live as a young adult. I was captain there, of the Broomfield's Secondary Modern School Rugby Team when I was about thirteen years old.

David, thirteen years old as captain of rugby team center-right in 1963

Rugby would keep me captivated for most of my adolescence, and of course, my enthusiasm has not slowed. It became a passion that I would never forsake. I remember one particularly challenging match in Warrington, where we battled against another local team. We were relentless rivals. The competition would be rough and thrilling. Everyone was over-stimulated about the fierce battle to be faced on the field between the teams. Adrenaline was at its peak, and everybody, including the spectators, was revved up for the match. As the clash of the gladiators progressed, fights broke out on the field, and tempers flared. In my final encounter in the game, while running the ball at pace, I was tackled and aggressively thrown against a six-foot wall (so much for friendly, sportsmanship). As I lifted my arm to protect my head, my arm was smashed against the substantially unmovable object and broke my humerus bone completely in two sections. I didn't see the humor at all, and the pain was almost unbearable. I needed an ambulance to rush me to hospital. I chuckle when I remember that the coach was more interested at the time in protecting my jersey from being cut during the initial repair procedure because of the high costs of rugby equipment and the low availability of funds. So much for socialistic ideals in the sports arena.

David on the Latchford-Albion Rugby Team 1975

I was fortunate to have a good life in this small, provincial but cherished environment even though there were indications of vicious political storms brewing from the clash of ideologies all around us in various hotspots in the United Kingdom.

In a quality of life survey done by the government of the United Kingdom as recently as 2009, Warrington ranked the lowest of 152 English regions in a series of Comprehensive Area Assessments that included public transport, public health, childhood obesity, and crime reduction. High unemployment rates were noted, as well as relatively low life expectancy[2].

I remember Burtonwood near to my home, which was a small village located on the outskirts of Warrington. Burtonwood was a strategic spot since both the Royal Air Force Base, and United States Army Air Force base was here. The RAF opened the base in 1940 in response to World War II, and in 1942, it became a strategic site for the United States of America for war operations. The base was home to 18,000 American military personnel at the close of the war.

Humphrey Bogart and Bob Hope came with various other stars to visit the Burtonwood in order to entertain the troops at what was then the largest US Army Air Force base outside of the United States.[3]. In 1946, the base was transferred back again to the United Kingdom. The United States continued to operate from the base on a smaller scale. The base closed officially in 1991. The government has demolished the runways and most buildings. RAF Burtonwood Heritage Centre is all that remains.[4]

I remember visiting the base on "open days" as a young lad, to have a look at the airplanes. I noticed back then that there was a considerable difference between the vehicles. It was obvious that the Americans were enjoying a different standard of living even after the war. Their vehicles were bigger, newer, shinier, and noticeably better in quality than those of my friends and their families. The bicycles that belonged to the locals, including my own, were all pieced together from discarded parts using rags to hold them in place. We creatively re-engineered those battered bikes to satisfy our needs to get around. The bicycle seats were anything but comfortable and sort of took the fun out of getting around on them. My dad, Jack, was a wizard at re-building a bicycle from different parts. He "refurbished" the seats by wrapping rags around whatever was left of the structure and then covering the whole thing with sackcloth from an old potato sack. You did not really have to worry much about someone stealing it. It was not long after that I knew that I wanted to live in an economy so prosperous that even the children enjoyed the latest models of shiny bicycles without rags to hold them together.

Even so, I was blessed to have the loving protection of those who cared for me as a child. I grew up in an area that was and still is strongly influenced by the welfare state policies. As I grew to adulthood, my life was a good one because I came from strong family ethics and values, but perhaps most impactful was the fact that I wanted it to be good. I set my thinking in that direction, but adventures were waiting ahead as they always are in our lives. I was yet to experience the most significant relationship that would impact me for the ages to come. There were good things ahead.

David and his mate Ian, age 18 in 1968

*Three*

# MEETING BARBARA

My love waits there in San Francisco
Above the blue and windy sea
When I come home to you, San Francisco,
Your golden sun will shine for me!

I Left My Heart in San Francisco

--Tony Bennett 1962

I came of age in Warrington and began enjoying spending time with my mates as we tried our skills at charming the local girls. Sometimes we did well, sometimes we crashed and burned, but we always enjoyed the thrill of the chase. One night, I met a girl at a local pub dance who was just a bit older. She was beautiful and stood out miles above the other girls. I had not yet established my skill as a charmer, and my courage was not at its peak. I decided the remedy was in a couple of beers that assisted me in asking her for a Christmas kiss even though it was just October. Fortunately for me, she laughed and then responded well to my request.

I got to walk her home that night. When we got to her house, I met her older brother and then realized that he worked at the same company as me. I also suddenly remembered that I had inflated my real age by a couple of years when I met Barbara, and I knew that my fibbing was about to be exposed by this older brother. Ronnie turned out to be a good friend through the years.

On our first date, I walked through the front door, and her first question was, "How old are you anyway?" I answered, with a little hesitation, "I am only sixteen. Do you want me to go?" She laughed and said she had already found me out, but she liked me anyway. I was over the moon. In the sixties, her favorite song was Tony Bennett's memorable rendition of "I Left My Heart in San Francisco." Barbara had been dreaming about a voyage to America even before we met.

We were married after three years in 1969 and made our home in Warrington, which is between Manchester and Liverpool. Liverpool was where the Beatles would start their phenomenal career. We were young people who found ourselves a part of the culture that produced the "Mersey Beat" that would give rise to the "British Invasion" of the sixties even though Barbara still preferred Tony Bennett at the time.

David and Barbara on an early date

David and Barbara on the front right in the
'Working Man's Club in 1970

It was here in the United Kingdom that we would raise our three amazing sons as I polished my trade and pursued my dreams of becoming an entrepreneur in England's rapidly changing post-industrial economy.

I was an apprentice engineer at an American subsidiary called Rubery Owen until the age of twenty-one. After finishing my apprenticeship, I couldn't see my future working in a factory as an engineer for the rest of my life and decided that I still wanted to move on to the bigger and better dreams I had imagined as a kid looking through the fence at Burtonwood. I took a job as an insurance salesman even though my workmates tried so extremely hard to dissuade me. They said that too many people were in sales and competition would be fierce. I had my mind and my heart set on the bigger and the better. During my first week in the sales force, I made more money than I had ever made in any week as an engineer.

David and Barbara Wedding Photo in 1969

David, Barbara, Simon, Philip and Ben

At the age of thirty-three, after living life on my terms away from God and following my ideas rather than the sound biblical wisdom that my parents had worked to instill in me, I was about to encounter something hugely bigger than I could have ever imagined. At that point in my life, I was determined that my plans were more conducive for the exciting life that I had planned for myself. I tried hard to run from the old and time-tested ideas of discipline, wisdom, moderation and most importantly, from faith in a Creator who knew and loved me so much better than I knew myself. On Sundays, I preferred to spend my mornings training for rugby with my teammates who also knew how to have the kind of fun that appealed to me. It seemed that fun became harder and harder to hold on to and I began to be convicted of my prideful and somewhat self-centered life that was, in fact, a sinful life. At the same time, my wife, Barbara was experiencing a life and heart-changing encounter with the Lord Jesus Christ. I watched her change into a person that I had not seen or known before her experience. I was a miserable grump, yet she was patient with me and prayed quietly and consistently. At first, I was angry and did not want anything to do with her newfound commitment and faith in a God that I had only, up until then, heard about from my parents. But I was curiously attracted to this God. I began to learn that a relationship with him through Jesus Christ was not only possible but was the goal of one's existence.

I began to spend hours working hard in my restaurant venture. I was doing well financially, but lacked the same remarkable joy that Barbara seemed to have. Something was missing and I knew that I could not be satisfied without finding out what it was. I knew there was something more than what life seemed to be offering me. I would go out with my rugby teammates and drinking friends, yet I still could not find that elusive contentment that I lacked.

God carried me to a point of intense conviction and distress until I finally decided to go to church with Barbara to find some peace. I really envied her joy but would be satisfied even with the peace of being in God's presence and in His house. Could that be possible for me? Then on a Sunday evening in July of 1983, after arguing with Barbara over nothing at all, I went to church to the fellowship that Barbara attended. While listening to the word of God that seemed to be directed at me personally,

I was hit hard. I began to reflect and thought of my life as I had fashioned it. I realized that I was, indeed, the sinner to whom the teachings of Jesus referred, full of pride and full of self. It was an unforgettable moment. I was heartbroken because of my foolish insistence on having my own way throughout my young life. I could not deny the truth that was surrounding me while clouds of doubt began to evaporate in the sun after a rainy day. I found myself in tears and moving toward the altar for prayer. I was ready for the life change that I knew I could not live without and I was truly born again that evening.

Life became even more exciting, more purposeful, our marriage was firmer, and for the first time our precious family unit was heading in the right direction. Now, both Barbara and I were joyful and giving praise to a God that loved us and that we both knew for ourselves. I was optimistic, happy, even excited about the future and what it would bring.

Barbara

Warrington was known mainly for its role in the history of England's industrialization with its considerable number of factories located in the area. A statue of Oliver Cromwell stands in front of the Warrington Academy. Cromwell was considered by many to be a remarkable statesman. Yet there has been much debate in the town over Cromwell's controversial practices and policies.

Warrington's predominately unionized, working-class citizens worked in the steel working, wire-making, coal-mining, and brewing industries where strikes were a regular occurrence. Rugby was a means of channeling the energy stored up by young men who worked long hours and hard shifts in the factories and the mines. Even though most of my rugby mates were left-leaning and socialistic in thought, we got along without problems because I was often the only conservative in the bunch. We could live together, and it probably even created balance in our community. We respected each other and could certainly relate to the shared experience of growing up in the northwest of England during the sixties, seventies, and eighties.

My mates came from hearty family units that were familiar with hard times as the United Kingdom struggled to recover from a costly and demanding war effort. Ours was a culture where the family was an important institution, and where friendships provided necessary and solid social foundations. We often enjoyed a laugh and a pint of beer shared after long, hard days. Yet because of financial hardships and the family strains that accompany these hardships, there were problems that hindered the realization or even the pursuit of life dreams and goals. There were not a lot of choices concerning what you could do with your life. Most young men were happy to have a job, start and provide for a family, and survive or evade hard times.

We tried to raise our sons to know to maintain a good work ethic and to work hard at achieving their goals. I wanted them to be their own persons, but not to be overcome using any substance that might be popular among their peers. I wanted them to have the ability to choose carefully for themselves. I tried to set the example by modeling moderation to them.

Fortunately, Barbara also had a strong hand in the boys becoming the men that they have become. She would be proud to look in on her family today. We tried to show them not to be afraid to try something different and to launch out into the deep. There is always something more than you can expect beyond your comfort zone. You should always expect good results for your efforts and faith in God. Persistence always pays off.

I love the song New York, New York by Frank Sinatra. He says "*if I can make it there, I'm gonna make it anywhere. It's up to you...*" That is what it's all about. It's up to you and you can't just depend on the government or any other organism or organization for a good foundation except the Lord Himself. *In God, We Trust* is the best motto to be found.

I had taken my lead from my father, Jack. These ideas were to be my blessing to my sons. It was their most precious inheritance coupled with the knowledge of Jesus Christ as a personal savior with whom they could have a deep relationship. What could be more crucial in helping them navigate troubled waters in an increasingly troubling world?

I continued to try out my entrepreneurial wings and develop my skills in several different venues. But I knew that I still wanted to succeed in the American *land of opportunity*. The times that probably were the most discouraging in my business ventures and explorations were facing problems with the tax programs such as the Value Added Tax or VAT. These kinds of taxes caused overburdening strain and sometimes resulted in the government cruelly winding up an established business.

Government power surrounding taxation was quite forceful in the United Kingdom and can still be frightening even today. The government holds the authority to completely shut down a business if the extra and seemingly exorbitant taxes are unpaid. I have several friends and acquaintances who have found themselves victims of this unpleasant experience of winding up.

In addition to tough circumstances for a young man, life in post-war England was a very different place for women than what is the norm in the United States. Most often, women stayed at home. Women were not even allowed in bars or pubs without being accompanied by a male. Things have changed considerably, but no place more profoundly over the centuries than here in the United States. It took me by surprise how enterprising and accomplished American women were. They reminded me of my mother, Charlotte.

*Four*

# COMING TO AMERICA

Only in America
Dreamin' in red white and blue
Only in America
Where we dream as big as we want to
We all get a chance
Everybody gets to dance
Only in America

Only in America

--Jay and the Americans 1965

As a young man with a wife and three children, I continued to work extremely hard at trying my entrepreneurial skills in several different venues. We took a wonderful family holiday to Florida in 1983. We rented a shiny, big American car and sunned on the beautiful white, sandy beaches and blue waters of the Gulf Coast. We explored as many beaches on the Atlantic Coast of Florida as possible, passed through the Everglades and the Okefenokee Swamp, galloped through the Disney parks, celebrated New Years in Key Biscayne near Miami, drove through the rest of the Keys, stopped in Fort Lauderdale and then explored Cape Canaveral and the Kennedy Space Center.

I decided on that trip, that the US was probably going to be the place where I would find the answer to my dream. I wanted my family to have opportunities to enjoy life to its fullest not just go from day to day trying to make a living without dreams, aspirations, or achievable goals. The pursuit of a new and different lifestyle would impact my thinking until I launched my hopes realizing one of my most persistent and important life-long goals.

I immigrated to America with my Barbara, my wife of thirty-one years, to start a new chapter in our lives during the last months of the 1990s and just ahead of the arrival of a new millennium. All the boys had emptied the nest, as the Americans call it. We spent months planning our new adventure after having agreed on a mutual goal. Making this huge transition and move was highly unusual for most people since we were a clan-oriented, close-knit group, and our families had probably been this way for centuries. Social mobility was exceedingly rare while moving to a new town let alone a country was almost never done.

We were fortunate enough to have another couple as particularly close friends who were younger and even more adventurous and who had already made the same move only a couple of years before us. Even so, our sons were just beginning their own families. Consequently, it was much more of a sacrifice, especially for Barbara. It was still our dream to spend the last part of our lives on soil quite different than where we had grown up. Barbara's exact words were, "I don't want to finish my life in Warrington." Somewhere away from the socialistically influenced north of England that we had known throughout our childhoods and most of our adult lives was a new start for us. Someone had said, "By leaving behind your old self and taking a leap of faith into the unknown, you find out what you're truly capable of becoming." I had always believed there were no rewards without risks. Of course, we had questions, but no fear strong enough to hold us back. People in England generally do not try launching out this far. Some of them do not even think about leaving the town where they were born. I am glad that I can say the trip is worth the leap, and faith in a God who leads makes all the difference. After visiting our old friends who had moved to Georgia ahead of us, we were ready to take the plunge.

We decided to proceed with our plans to leave the community, our comfort zone, for a place that would give us opportunities beyond what we had dreamed of when we were young people in the years of the fifties, sixties, and seventies. The United States held a promise of a different dynamic. Things certainly seemed to move more slowly back at home, and people also seemed to settle into older age more quickly. In England, I remembered as a young man talking to a friend who was in his fifties who was planning to move to a new house. I thought at the time that he was certainly too old to be thinking about doing that.

We set off excitedly, on our new adventure with "great expectations" for the future. As we went forward with our plans, we were full of energy and anticipation since we had enjoyed Florida and Caribbean vacations with the children when they were young. We settled in Atlanta, Georgia. Georgia is one state away from the Florida beaches.

When we got to Atlanta, it sizzled and sparkled under warm, sunny skies that were so much different from the rainy, cold, and gray ones that we had lived under for most of our lives. Since our close friends had moved ahead of us and had already set up housekeeping there, they would assist us in making the transition from the United Kingdom to the United States. They were eager to have some "family" to join them here. These friends recall a story from times before they made their move to relocate to the US. He was a friend, a partner in business, and an entrepreneur himself. They were also followers and believers in Jesus Christ and had been members of the same church congregation where we belonged in Warrington. One day a member of the church prayed out loud for him and his family to have favor and be blessed financially. At the time, it seemed reasonable and even humble to pray this way, but on looking back, the socialistic mentality of many of the church members was evident. Their prayers reflected the thinking that seemed to be centered on themselves and on their own interests. After coming to America and finding a church home, my friends noted the prayer from the pastor for the people. He prayed for favor and blessings to be able to bless the entire church. The pastor was modeling the better idea of praying for more benefits and blessings for others rather than just for you. There was even capitalism in the realization that you cannot help others or anyone without the necessary finances. We immediately noticed the incredible work ethic that the Americans demonstrated. It was evident that they worked hard and expected to be rewarded well for their labours.

We were surprised to meet many people in America who were well into middle age and still moving to new homes, sometimes across the country. Many of them were undertaking new business ventures. Some were even going back to earn higher degrees of education. I was impressed since doing those kinds of projects and exploring new territories was considered strange in the UK. America was a land filled with an abundance of choices and opportunities. The promise of a life without restrictions was a welcome change, and we were eager to accept it.

We began to frequent the church that our friends suggested. We joined a large and gifted choir complete with orchestra and contemporary musicians, all directed by a talented young man who had a knack for choosing just the right praise and worship music that made our new adventure even more exciting. It helped us to begin making lasting and precious friendships on this side of the ocean. What stimulating praise and worship we enjoyed at the church! The messages were insightful and uplifting. We had found our church home that made the transition complete.

It was a challenge to transfer to a new business mindset that was quite different from the one that we had known in the UK. It was a bit daunting at first. It felt like I was watching an amazingly fast and competitive race going by in front of me. I knew that to survive and accomplish anything, I would have to get myself in gear, jumping into the race with all that I could muster, and then keep up to the lively but stimulating pace. Keep up! It seemed like everybody whizzing past me had the advantage of being born into the race. I knew that I had to find something inside me that had been deposited along the way, something that I didn't even know that I had. If I could make it here, I could make it anywhere. I took the challenge because I knew who I was created to be. I knew the God who had made and called me to just this moment at just this time. That knowledge was more powerful than any other background experience. I knew that I would keep pushing until I was running alongside the best of them and with persistence, that is exactly what I've done.

Another favorite hymn was Richard Smallwood's *Total Praise*. Joining the choir had turned out to be a brilliant decision and we were glad that we made the cut. There was something very uplifting and even supernatural about singing praises each week, something that strengthened my resolve, reaffirmed my purpose, and caused me to look higher instead of just looking around me for courage.

Lord, I will lift my eyes to the hills
Knowing my help is coming from You
Your peace You give me in time of the storm
You are the source of my strength
You are the strength of my life
I lift my hands in total praise to You

Total Praise

--Richard Smallwood 1990

We tried to make the trip across the pond as often as possible to visit. It was a challenge since our loved ones were an ocean away. There certainly was a different *rhythm*. We could sense the beating of a resoundingly different drum. We chuckled with each other after hearing "mispronunciations" of common words in the English language like *aluminium*. The Americans were calling it *aluminum foil*. Although we technically shared a common language, it was not always easy to realize it. We laughed a lot between ourselves. Since we were in the Deep South, there were charming accents, and some were not charming at all. Sometimes they were impossible to catch, and there were even dialects to be translated in addition to a colorful, new vocabulary to be mastered. Happy Christmas became Merry Christmas.

Even though we really missed the children and especially Olivia, our first grandchild so far, we found ourselves welcomed into a warm group of Atlantans surrounding us with American style hospitality and warm affection. The holidays that we were not able to spend in England were at least busily, filled with rehearsals, services, shopping, performances, and social events. It was all very stimulating, sometimes even hectic. Still, we navigated the waters of assimilation that had expanded considerably in many ways and narrowed in others since the Americans had thrown that first tea party in honor of King George.

We felt like we were living our dream and seemed to be on a perpetual vacation. We enjoyed a rejuvenating but busy *honeymoon* period as we made our transition. There were so many differences, yet so many similarities. America was so near to us, yet so far away. We learned to accept and appreciate new attitudes and expressions like *fixin to do something*. We tasted newfound foods like grits, biscuits, and gravy. As we heard fascinating tales of families that had been here through so many different generations and lengths of time, we began to enjoy the southern and American way of life.

We also began to eat out to try the southern hospitality at local restaurants and were amazed at how quickly and with great care that the wait staff willingly showered their clients. What a hustle for them as they crowded the open kitchens and competed to get their orders filled by the chefs! Now we understood much better what all those American tips were. There was not such a system in British or European restaurants. The bill includes the gratuity for service, so for the waiters and waitresses that we were used to, hurrying and excellent service were not to be rewarded. Why bother?

We eventually realized that we had, along with our American neighbors, maintained a mutual fascination over the centuries since we had parted ways. Even with all the excitement, we still missed the children and thought of them often. We knew there would be exciting days ahead and even more thrilling discoveries as we learned the cultural landscape. Doors were opening in the natural and spiritual realm. I was coming to understand that I needed more than ever to depend on God and on myself rather than looking for a handout.

Barbara began to experience episodes related to an undiagnosed heart condition within a year of arrival. We were somewhat relieved since we believed that the American medical system was a strong one. While delivering packages to the Post Office to be mailed, Barbara collapsed and was rushed to a hospital several miles away. After the doctor's review, it was considered life-threatening and possibly a brain aneurism. The doctors decided to transport her to a specialist unit in Atlanta in a helicopter where she was in ICU. They worked hard to revive her over several days. She had been incoherent and unsure of what had happened to her. The medical attention she received was impressive. She recovered after a week or so, but still suffered from some problems until about a month later. She was able to continue her life for the most part.

Almost exactly a year after the first event, Barbara had a second event. This time it was a massive heart attack. She slipped away in the early hours of the morning. I lost Barbara after only being in the US for a total of eighteen months. I was devastated. Barbara was my first love, my partner in this still very new adventure. I considered going back to the United Kingdom. I was fortunate enough to have already established a support system of good friends and church leaders who surrounded me here.

Barbara and I had been very much involved in the music program and group at the Mount Paran Church of God in Atlanta, Georgia. The pastoral staff and so many concerned and amazing people in the choir offered me strong support. I was also grateful for my dear friends who had come to America before us.

I missed Barbara so very much but knew that she was with the Lord in heaven. That knowledge was encouraging giving me the strength to go on. I knew that I would see her again. Perhaps the most challenging task that I have ever had to do was to tell our sons that their mother was gone. I have no idea where I found the courage to do so alone, but I am convinced that strength was given me by a God who loved me more than words could express even amid my unbearable loss. I also knew that I was not completely alone. There were so many genuine and sincere people who reached out to me with care and concern. I will always remember the love, support, and care they gave me while I searched for healing and answers.

I knew that I needed to continue going forward rather than going back to the old way of life that I had known before. I knew that Barbara would have wanted me to keep going forward. I knew that my sons were hurting because they lost their mother and that our lives would never be the same. I knew that it would not be any less, but probably more difficult without Barbara. I could sense the presence of the Lord and the reassurance that even though things would be different, there was still a bright future ahead for all of us. I believed that my future and my goal of living in "the land of opportunity" was a valid one. I took a long deep breath, gathered all my courage, and continued my pursuit of that "American dream" that I had contemplated throughout my life.

Some days seemed incredibly lonely. I would not have made it at all without my faith in a God who is real and whose hand had been evident throughout my whole existence. My English and American friends and family on both sides of the Atlantic seemed to be being used by God to care for and love me as if they were His strong, comforting arms and hands working here on earth. I knew that heaven would come one day and that I would see Barbara again. This thought gave me the most comfort. Now I only had to convince the boys. There were mountains to climb and battles to be fought and won in the here and now.

> America, America
> God shed His grace on Thee
> And crown thy good, with brotherhood
> From sea to shining sea!

> America The Beautiful

> --Katharine Lee Bates 1895

*Five*

# HOME AT LAST

Hallelujah, home at last
Joy forever, sorrows past
All of heaven waits
As the Bride comes through the gate
Hallelujahs fill the air, home at last!

Home At Last

--Geron Davis

I remember the night of Wednesday choir rehearsal when the director, Mark, had someone call me to listen on the phone shortly after Barbara went home to be with the Lord. The choir had recently recorded a gospel album, and they were singing one of my favorite hymns recorded on the album. It was *Home At Last* written by Geron Davis. It tells the story of the halls of heaven and the plans for a great and glorious homecoming with the angels waiting for the Lord to give the call for that great day of rejoicing with music filling the air. The words are amazingly prophetic and filled with the hope of incredibly triumphant expectations as the church finally makes it home.

Time went by rather slowly as it does with these kinds of situations. Yet, I knew that the One who loved me with an everlasting love, the Lord Jesus was near to me. I felt His reassurance and His urging to trust Him. I felt as if there was work to be done.

I realized that I had a calling here in the *land of the free and the home of the brave*. It wasn't always clear, but I knew my Lord was there compelling me to go forward and to press on. Even though I still missed Barbara by my side and her sweet encouragement, I knew that she would want me to see it through, to go after my dream. I had time to reflect even more on my life and what it meant to trust a God that I could not see, but I knew he was leading me to a marvelous end.

One of my favorite movies was *The Preacher's Wife* with Whitney Houston and Denzel Washington. Washington plays an angel who has been sent from God to assist an inner-city preacher struggling to hold his church, community, and family together. The wife, played by the incredible songstress, Whitney Houston, sang a deeply moving rendition of *I Love the Lord* with such an unbelievable conviction that reminded me that I could count on His attentiveness to my every cry. Even today, I try to reflect beyond my ability to understand the strength of His love and protection whenever I hear the song based on Psalm 116: 11. There is never a dry eye in the room when someone plays this song by Houston. In the end, she hastens to His throne and knows that there is a place for us there.

> I love the Lord
> He heard my cry
> And pitied every groan
> Long as I live
> When troubles rise
> I'll hasten to His throne, I'll hasten to His throne, I'll hasten to His throne!

> I Love the Lord

> --Whitney Houston 1996

I knew without a doubt that I was not alone, that I could go anytime to His throne, and that I would be welcomed whenever life gets overwhelming. I knew I could find strength there. I knew that even though the most disheartening thing that could have happened to me in saying goodbye to Barbara would always be troublesome to understand, I had a reassurance that I would have never known without the trying circumstances of being without her. It is surprising how trials produce eternal fruit that no other situation can produce. I knew the Lord was leading me and giving me courage.

Even though I missed Barbara every waking day, I felt that I was at home in this new land. It was suited to my personality and my aspirations. I tried to enjoy being here, even just driving through the city, especially at night, seeing the growing number and size of skyscrapers that filled the Atlanta downtown night sky.

Persistence, determination, and encouragement were necessary tools for success that I had relied on in the past, and I needed those tools more than ever. I know them to be the pillars that will always support a life well-lived and produce a job well-done. I knew that my encouragement would most often come from myself as I remembered the scripture command to *"build yourself up on your most holy faith and praying in the Holy Spirit"* from Jude 1: 20 AMP.

One day one of my closest friends asked after several long months if there was anyone that I might want to take out. There was someone that I thought of, someone also in the choir, but in an honest conversation with God, I carefully explained that I had been with Barbara so long that there was NO WAY that I was going to ask any other woman to go out with me. I reminded Him that I just didn't know how to do that so, I further informed the God of the universe that He would have to have the woman ask me out, that He would have to do the arranging. Lynette happened to be an International Flight Attendant for Delta Airlines and had been to my part of the U.K. several times while working and laying over in Manchester. Just a few weeks after my conversation, she asked me if I'd like to go to the theatre. Some people in the choir were going as a group, but her flying schedule was inconvenient to join them, so Lynette asked if I'd like to accompany her there. It turned out that she was the lady that I had in mind when my friend asked me sometime earlier. Of course, I had never shared the name with anyone. Lynette had often stood next to Barbara during rehearsal, and they chatted, shared family pictures of precious children, and would have probably been friends if Barbara had lived. One night at choir rehearsal before Barbara went home to be with the Lord, during moments when neighbor chatting didn't interfere with rehearsing,

Barbara asked Lynette if she had ever been married. Her response was, "No, not yet but I'm thinking that I'm ready, Barbara. Would you pray for me for that right guy?" Barbara went home and informed me of the conversation, told me that Lynette was one of the kindest persons she had met here, and so we prayed for her to find the right guy.

Barbara's death was a blow for Lynette at the time since she had just lost her father a few months earlier. It all seemed to come out of nowhere. She felt like she and Barbara would have been great friends if they had the opportunity. It almost felt like Barbara had set things up to make it easier for me, as if she knew more than seemed possible. I only know that Barbara loved me very much and I loved her.

> If I fell in love with you
> Would you promise to be true?
> And help me understand
> Cause I've been in love before
> And I found that love is more
> than just holding hands.

If I Fell

--Paul McCartney, The Beatles, 1964

I sensed the Lord leading me to marry Lynette and within months, I was married again. We now live in a suburb south of Atlanta where we still enjoy planning and continue to dream about a productive future of adventures shared in both the United Kingdom, since my sons and their growing families still live throughout the U.K. and the United States. We love to travel throughout the world and do so as often as we can. One of my sons reminded me that living with an American wife might not be quite as simple as living with his mother who was an English lady. I soon found out that he was right when I asked her to make me a cup of tea. She was busily working on a project, and swiftly informed me "that you have two legs and can jolly well do it for yourself."

David and Lynette wedding photo 2001

The blessing for me was that Lynette and I enjoyed spending time together with the Lord, reading His Word for insight and revelation, then going to that throne room in prayer just as Barbara and I had enjoyed doing when we first came to America. We continued to sing praises to the God we knew and loved as we reflected on His glory in the Mount Paran Church Choir. Singing praises to God is the most direct route to being in His presence. Being lifted to the heavens in worship is such a thrilling experience! We are both so grateful to have had the chance to do so.

Atlanta inspired in me a sense of adventure and excitement as I moved about the city from one area to the next, growing more familiar with and settling into the American lifestyle. The city life was exhilarating with its southern charm, numerous conventions, sports complexes, busy airport, and bustling Merchandise Mart. It was big enough to push me out of any provincial small-town feeling that might have been left over from life in the English countryside yet not so big that I would be overwhelmed with the American hustle and bustle. There was a hum of success in the air as I drove down West Paces Ferry with its beautiful dogwood trees poised along the driveways and situated near the facades of millionaire occupied mansions.

Not too far away, just a few hours ride in the car were delightful beach spots and vacation condos, available should you need a quick escape to the sun-washed beaches, the stunning, blue waters, and the dazzling white sands of the southern shores in nearby Florida.

We fell in love with the South Carolina Island called Hilton Head with its world-class marina, its red and white striped lighthouse, and its charming army of international student interns studying hospitality at the resorts and restaurants. We met several from Manchester happy to chat about their experiences in the US. The weather was always pleasantly accommodating and especially during spring. Everything everywhere was in full bloom. If you were looking for scorching, hot summers that seemed like heaven to someone like me who had spent too many days in the northern English landscape and weather, then Atlanta, Georgia was the place to be. I was a passionate sun-chaser from way back when and would always be one.

David returning from surfing at Diamond Head in Hawaii in 2001

*Six*

# WHAT'S GOING ON?

Mother, mother, there's too many of you crying.
Brother, brother, brother, there's far too many of you dying.
You know we've got to find a way
To bring some loving here to stay!

Oh, picket lines and picket signs
Don't punish me with brutality.
me on, Talk to me so you can see
What's going on, tell me what's going on yeah, I'll tell you what's going on?

What's Going On
--Marvin Gaye 1971

After some twenty years of living here in the United States, I still refer to it as the *land of opportunity*, even if that sounds like a cliché in today's world. I come from a country and culture that was very restrictive. The opportunities were limited for those of us in the northwest of England unless you were fortunate enough to have unlimited resources. However, I am beginning to hear the clamoring demand for what I know to be potentially dangerous and devastating changes to the American landscape because of the pursuit and incorporation of similar ideologies and resulting behaviors that I witnessed in post-war England. I am observing increasing numbers of young, American families struggling under economic distress disgruntled by unfulfilled opportunities for themselves and even increasingly, limited ones for their children. There is growing concern over seemingly, limited and dwindling abilities needed to provide their children with the essentials and preparation necessary for success in a highly competitive world marketplace.

The public-school system seems to be guilty of misinterpreting and failing to convey information vital to civic responsibility. Ultimately, the responsibility lies with the parents who no longer want to bother to teach ethics, values, or even morals to their children, yet want to hold the overburdened and undervalued teachers of the American Public Schools Systems responsible for "raising" their children. At the same time, the teachers are squeezed or forced into unsustainable work environments filled with frustration and dwindling resources. In an attempt to correct and "re-write" history, there is a noticeable and perhaps intentional ignorance about the things that matter most. From my perspective, socialism and extreme liberal ideology are both high on the list of things to be learned so as not to repeat deadly mistakes that my culture made during the post-war years of austerity measures.

For those who were not around to witness the exploits of Cold War politics, the abhorrent policies of socialism and communism, and then enticed by government promises of "free" everything, it becomes difficult for them to refuse, sort of like offering ice cream cones to unsuspecting children. However, those same tasty-looking treats instantly deteriorate and take on a nightmarish quality after being ingested.

We have firsthand experience hearing the forceful liberal agenda and socialistic ideology presented on most college campuses in the United States. Lynette began teaching at the college and university level after going back to do graduate work following early retirement from Delta Air Lines. She witnessed the evidence of growing unrest and continuing ideological changes so prevalent on university campuses and even in the classrooms. The attack on the conservative culture was usually subtle but developed more and more rigorously as the years went by. Soon, the students could hardly tolerate any differences of opinion expressed by those who did not always agree with the liberal majority there. The democratic process was seemingly about to be replaced with something else, something unrecognizable.

I remember vivid demonstrations in the northwest of England that expressed a dangerous kind of dissent. I recognized the changes in the air towards radical thinking and practices leaning to the left and far away from traditional values of right and wrong. I experienced the deterioration of work ethics and ethics in general as I watched neighborhoods become like war zones because of increasing crime rates, high unemployment, and a "don't care" attitude creeping over towns in the welfare state of the northwest of England. It was a process that had been brewing since the indoctrination of the Labour government mentality after WWII.

I have observed these situations and heard conversations for myself. I understand that hard conditions and ideas have also been part of American history for young students, for minorities, and for all groups of people struggling to assimilate and find their part of that "American pie". I am watching things rapidly change in America. Some changes are positive, some not at all good, as more and more people from different backgrounds, many of them are wanting to re-create the cultures from which they immigrated rather than embracing the benefits of a new perspective. They are responding by clamoring to push forward socialistic ideology in the name of *progress*, and in an attempt to fill the void for themselves and their children. I am watching the American public enticed to buy into what I have known to be unrealistic theories based on holding someone else responsible or blaming someone else for disintegrating opportunities and circumstances. The same ones want "free" healthcare and education without stopping to realize that you always get what you pay for or at least what you strive for in terms of quality. Who will bear the cost and what exactly will be the cost? Someone must pay. A significant, growing number of people are now willing and ready to consider American socialism without even a clear understanding of how that will look and what it means. It represents a different way of life due to the promise of those irresistible "free" goods. Politicians and unethical, power-driven opportunists are promising to fill those unfulfilled dreams using multiple, insupportable schemes.

In theory, it's all a wonderfully dreamy world. I have lived through the reality and the aftermath of large-scale government involvement which resulted in organized rationing of foodstuffs, clothing, and fuel that led directly to the state's growing acceptance of responsibility for and power over the lives of its citizens and its resulting increase of burdensome taxation. The increased government expenditures soon deteriorated into socialistic nightmares that included extreme taxes on every *luxury,* albeit inferior quality item that offered even minor distractions to its citizens as a respite from growing discouragement. Quality products were hardly attainable and often impossible to find.

I remember when Barbara and I came to America and shopped at the "bargain" stores that were still big-name businesses in the US like Marshall's. It quickly became one of my favorites because I could find brand name clothing from good manufacturers at great prices. The comparable store in the UK was TK Maxx, and the quality of the products sold there was not at all equal. I could have never found things that well made in England that we left for the kinds of prices that we were paying here in America. And we haven't even begun to talk about the electronic items or big-ticket items like automobiles that were so heavily taxed that made them difficult to purchase. I could not forget Burtonwood and the bicycles of my childhood.

An eye-opening, example of an already deteriorating socialistic and bureaucracy-burdened institution is the American public school system that I mentioned earlier. Before coming to the United States, I recall friends and relatives talking about how far below average the schools were, and I wanted to defend the Americans. Yet on looking at the system and its failings that have produced a pervasive ignorance about what socialism is among other failings, I have heard it called "the American anti-education system." According to an article in the *Business Insider* on September 27, 2018, the US has seen a marked decline in educational attainment. It states the reason for this decline as being the result of reduced and poorly allocated funding for key levels of public-school education. Statistics from the Pew Research Center rate American schools in thirty-eighth place out of seventy-one countries in math scores and twenty-fourth place in science. [5]

These numbers indicate a serious lack of responsible direction in general for a system in need of a fresh perspective and a lesson in relevancy. The lag that places them behind so many other nations clearly demonstrates a flawed system in terms of performance outcomes. Of all the institutions that are pertinent to society, public schools are among the most important, yet there has been a marked decline in those school systems as more bureaucratic ideas have taken hold. There is not enough focus on the performance of the students and too much focus on making sure there is government funding regardless of how poorly these systems continue to lag in producing quality educations for all. The hope of keeping pace with countries that do provide good and competitive quality education is becoming less and less of a reality.

I came of age during England's period of nationalization of necessary services. Simultaneously we saw the institutionalization of systems such as the so-called "free" National Health Service, to supply basic needs. England entered this era marked by the introduction of radical changes starting after WWII, progressing through the sixties, and finally extending through to the eighties. The United Kingdom, although it is considered a free-market economy, is still under the influence of various socialistic ideologies conceived in a search for a better life for its citizens.

I was born in 1949, shortly after the end of WWII. At that time various social measures were put into effect by the government to ease financial burdens and aid the people in recovering from stringent, living conditions brought on by the rationing of goods. These measures were designed and established to temporarily assist the general population with the cost of living necessities and expenditures. My parents were grateful for this type of assistance, and I remember that luxuries as a child were few and far between. At the age of five, my siblings and I had to share one candy bar, a Mars bar as I remember, cut into five pieces with our parents as a treat for the family once a week. We each had only one bite, and we did everything we could to make it last for five minutes by slowly taking ridiculously tiny morsels. I remember my father's attitude. He was grateful for anything after having had to endure the adversities of two World Wars during his lifetime. It was an admirable quality that would always be a part of my father's remembrance.

As I passed through my childhood years, into young adolescence and on to adulthood, I witnessed the transition from complete government control of goods and services such as housing, healthcare, and transportation to the eventual emergence of free enterprise, privatization, and the establishment of individual business developments. There was a glimmer of hope. Nationalization of the country's major services as the accepted means of business was changing. Margaret Thatcher voted in as Prime Minister in 1980 was the first to use the phrase *put the great back*. She would represent a change in government to bring about that end. Her goal was to put the *great* back into Great Britain.

45

*Seven*

# WHAT IS SOCIALISM?

Flew in from Miami Beach BOAC
Didn't get to bed last night
On the way the paper bag was on my knee
Man I had a dreadful flight
I'm back in the U.S.S.R.
You don't know how lucky you are boy
Back in the U.S.S.R.

Back in the U.S.S.R.

--The Beatles 1968

Socialism is an economic system or theory in which the government, rather than private enterprise, controls the production and distribution of goods substantially and in which cooperation instead of competition guides economic activity. Claude Henri de Rouvroy, Comte de Saint-Simon was a French economic and political theorist who greatly influenced sociology, politics, economics, and the philosophy of science during the early 1800s in France. The use of the word *socialism* was introduced by Saint-Simon, who would eventually refer to it as *utopian socialism* and as a contrast to *individualism* that focused on the moral value of the individual. These early socialists rejected the idea of *individualism* due to its failure to target the important social aspects of the Industrial Revolution. According to Saint-Simon and his cronies, individualism did not adequately address the concerns of poverty, of society based on competition, pervasive inequalities of wealth, and, finally, the subject of oppression.[6] He developed a political and economic ideology that would address the needs of a working class of individuals that included a wide range of people employed both manually and in all kinds of productive work directed at making a beneficial contribution to society.[7]

It is notable for our writings that Saint-Simon believed there was another group of people to whom he referred to as the *idling class* that consisted of those who wanted only to enjoy the benefits of other's work and to avoid working at all. He wanted to use meritocracy as the basis for a hierarchical merit-based system of managers and scientists who would be the leaders responsible for making government decisions.[8] It was sad to watch people among my peers, who were, in fact, very talented and quite intelligent become a part of anything so negatively referred to as the idling class. Yet talent can be easily squandered, and creative ability can be discouraged in those who have little or no options.

Saint-Simon had substantial criticism for expanded government intervention into the economy and said that the power of government should be to guard against anything that would hinder productive work and reduce idleness.

John Stuart Mill was a nineteenth-century philosopher and economist, also considered to have had considerable influence in the history of classical liberalism. Mill was an avid admirer of Henri Saint-Simon and his ideology. Mill believed that liberty, by definition, "justified the freedom of the individual as opposed to unlimited state and social control."[9] J.S. Mill and the *reformed liberals* of this era were thus proponents of a minimum of political regulation. Yet they agreed with their opponents that the signs on the road to equality and prosperity should indicate a maximum of free markets and a minimum of state interference.

For those of us living in the Labour government and welfare state communities, free markets would give us hope of a different kind of future, one that we could be proud of and look forward to for our children. Where, when, and how did the change from their initial concerns enter the development of massive government control?

Several liberal theorists followed those early ideologies, modifying and redefining the original ideas to fit their political agendas not unlike the constant fluctuations and rearrangement of ideas in the political arena of today.

*The Oxford English Dictionary* defines socialism as, "a political and economic theory of social organization which advocates that the means of production, distribution, and exchange should be owned or regulated by the community as a whole". *Dictionary.com* similarly defines socialism as, "a theory or system of social organization that advocates the vesting of the ownership and control of the means of production and distribution [of said goods], in the community as a whole." The problem with the success and efficiency of a socialistic government is that it must be based on the non-existent, idealistic, utopian society rather than on one that takes into account the habits and actual behaviors of human nature as portrayed through the history of mankind. In a feeble attempt to explain what is needed and to encourage people to seek the good of the community rather than the good of the individual, socialist ideologist suggest that the true basic nature of people is cooperative.

Our corner of the United Kingdom was centered on our shared experiences and therefore a shared identity. But never was there a drive to cooperate based on the absence of competition. Competition had always been a huge part of the culture and the battle was certainly fought in the sports arenas. There were considerable distinctions according to attitudes among the tribal groups of people of the northwest of England. You could go five miles in any direction and find yourself facing a completely different *tribe* of people who had completely different accents, habits, and families. They were waiting to fight you to prove their superiority. When I was a young lad, my family moved at least three times, and each time I had to fight and win to protect myself from bullies since I was the new kid. I learned to be tough and to stand up for myself. There certainly was no welcome committee to make sure that I would have pleasant assimilation. Each different community had its own rules and its tribe members were tough to confront.

In addition to the competition among *tribes*, there was the class system that has been so deeply ingrained in the culture and mindset of the people in the United Kingdom. If you found yourself out of your territory, there were many ways to wind up in more trouble than you might bargain on during any summer's evening.

I remember one evening at the Co-op Dance Hall. In order to avoid the gangs that waited outside the hall after the dance, you had to be leaving with a girl and even then, it was no guarantee that you were safe from a fight. This night, I hadn't seen anybody that I want to accompany so I left. I was wearing my white Mod jacket. The Mods and the Rockers were the two groups all over the country who hated each other. I wasn't actually in the group, but I liked to dress in the best and most stylish clothes like the Mods if I could. The other guys came from rough areas of the town and were usually the ones waiting to beat up somebody. That evening, as I walked out, the gang had gathered and was waiting to pounce on me as I walked by in my white jacket. I stood out like the moon and of course, the gang followed. I felt someone grab my coat from behind and I used my rugby skills and hit his hand hard from off my back. As I knocked his hand off, I heard someone shout, "Let's get him! "There were about twenty or so that I would have had to fight. They were angry kids, always in trouble with the police and would have made short work of me. I ran like the wind passing all my friends with their dates. No one volunteered to help me since they were all with their girls. One of my workmates shouted, "take your _____ white coat off! They can see you too easily." I kept running as fast as I could and again was glad of my rugby training. I managed to get around a corner and take off the jacket. I quickly folded it, and then I hid it at the back of the British Legion building.

It was critical to be able to think on your feet since this kind of gang behavior was a frequent occurrence in the dance halls. There was not even any alcohol to get them started. A fight was what they came for, and it did not matter at all that there were girls. Sometimes the girls from the neighborhoods were right there fighting with the guys. One little thing could set off a violent confrontation. These were tough kids from tough backgrounds. The sad part was that they would carry this tribal aggression on to full bloom war-like mentality in adulthood. The sports stadium would become the battleground where the unbridled fighting between the opposing fans would continue in deadly confrontations.

I never told my parents what went on among the angry kids who had nothing else to do since many of them were born into abusive homes where alcoholic fathers made sure that their lives were even more severe. The gangs were looking for someone to abuse in return. It was a very rough time in my life and for all the young people from sound family structures who were trying to find the all-important peer acceptance that teenagers need. I remember walking home one evening past a house where two brothers were fighting in the street and were being egged on to bash each other well by the parents and other siblings. Everyone in the neighborhood was watching with excited curiosity. Even at the age of ten, I was amazed to see human beings from the same family wanting to bash each other's heads.

There was tremendous animosity and jealousy when mixing the various groups of kids. It was a brutal environment to grow up in, and the fact that we survived was a testimony to God's ability to care for me. I now know well at this point in my life that He had a plan for me. We had to live by our wits, but it was clear on looking back that God was watching over me closely.

Reflecting on some of my decisions, I was not sure at the time that I was doing the right thing. Even playing rugby caused me to wonder if I had made the right choices. I was captain of the soccer team when I was about thirteen. I was only a junior player, but they put me in the senior team because I was skilled. Later, during my apprenticeship at Rubery Owens, they asked me to play for their local soccer team since they were at the top of the league. The day I went to play, it was as if something was keeping me from performing well. I had never played so badly and just decided to leave and continue to play rugby. It was as if there was a plan in place, and as if there were angels on the pitch. Something was preventing me from playing soccer. I believe that God has always had a plan for my life and yours. It began to be more and more evident to me as I continued down the road of life. Someone was watching. I was being cared for by someone immensely powerful who loved me.

The socialist ideologists further assert that capitalism and feudalism have handicapped the evolution of society and that basic human nature has yet to emerge. It is as if capitalism for them is some genetic monster that has overwhelmed human nature since Adam and Eve or if you follow socialism's anti-biblical theories, since the big bang.[10]

One unforgettable story that I remember around this time was about a certain rugby player who was becoming professional at the age of seventeen. He was offered a sum of 3000 GBP as a signing fee by one of the professional clubs, plus a car and an extra job with the town council.

It was an amazing offer at the time. However, another professional club, after hearing the first offer, decided to offer the boy the same package but included a job for his father with the council as well. The young man's father directed his son to sign for the first offer because the father did not want to go to work. He was happy to continue getting his unemployment. The DOLE was the way to go since he could also keep his little jobs on the side and not have to report his income for taxes. These kinds of stories are still occurring frequently today.

An even more ominous problem presents itself with the phrase *controlled substantially by the government* or *cooperation rather than competition guiding economic activity*. The assumption here is that the government itself and its proponents are always trustworthy and dependable, allowing for no mistakes, corruption, or unethical behavior. Socialism is a political and economic theory of social organization that advocates the means of production, distribution, and exchange should be owned or regulated by the community as a whole through substantial state control. By this definition, it is a system that directs its adherents to rely wholly upon the group or state rather than promoting individual development, thus restricting the potential for maximum personal success. In a free-market economy, the consumer has the power and can *vote* with the amount of money he chooses to spend on the items available at competitive prices.

However, a socialist economy automatically gives the ultimate power and authority to the government. The elite leadership at the top of the chain has the overriding power to decide not only what the people should have, but also, how much they should pay for it. The people are not free to make decisions about what they want to buy, and they have no control over whether or not it is even available.

What is genuinely concerning is that in the so-called model socialist economies, shortages regularly occur, and the government runs out of necessary items. [11] We lived with these shortages in the United Kingdom and we learned that these are the required restrictions of life under austerity measures. We did not know any different since I spent my childhood in the years after WWII. Only the chosen few had access to whatever they think they might desire while everyone else must wait or make do with poor substitutes of horrible quality and quantity. Those in the lower working classes in the United Kingdom would certainly not qualify as the chosen few. Even though I developed this mindset as a result of indoctrination into acceptance of our status in the social hierarchy, I knew that I would live and think differently someday.

What happened to the slogan *for the benefit of the community as a whole*? Who could forget the high demand for toilet paper and other quantities of unusually abnormal numbers of items the world over as people tried to prepare for radical stay at home measures during a potentially deadly, pandemic?

While every socioeconomic theory is subject to interpretation by varying groups of political proponents, there are eight types of socialism, each differing in its attempt to emphasize how capitalism can best be modified to address the goals of the group. It is most understandable, then that confusion is a problem for a poorly informed and therefore easily influenced group of people. Full comprehension of socialistic theories and applications can be a daunting prospect.

Those who favor a socialistic type of government now include people who identify themselves as Christian. Christian Socialists would seek to make socialistic economics and political ideology more relevant than understanding the intention of God's laws and precepts and thus understanding that the nature of human beings is flawed, not because of capitalism but because of a sinful nature. It is for this reason that we need a savior who is Jesus Christ. According to the word of God, this is the reason He came into the world.

Socialists believe that the overarching moral issue of society is encapsulated in economics, politics, and science. This idea alone would disqualify any person who follows Jesus Christ from a seat at the socialistic table since materialism is the foundation of the socialistic theory as interpreted by Karl Marx, considered as the father of socialism. Since Marx held firmly to the belief that matter was a creative power, there was no longer a need for a creator God and certainly not for a savior who would sacrifice His life so that we may approach a holy God. Marx and his co-designers of socialistic thought conveniently eliminated any authority, apart from the state, leaving moralistic interpretations about how people should *do unto others* a matter of personal view. Socialism and its precepts, as understood among the rules of economic theory, easily fit in the category of legalized theft since the group has a right by law to the wealth of the individual, even though this individual probably worked hard for it.

An American friend recently submitted a poster on Facebook that seemed to sum things up in a way that was easy to grasp. It was a picture of Lenin with words across explaining, "*Socialism is Communism for slow learners.*" Perhaps there is more truth than fiction in his quip since the early distinction between the two philosophies was that communism directed its goals towards the socialization of production, as well as consumption. Socialism primarily aimed to impact production. What is remarkably notable is that after the Bolshevik Revolution of 1917, Vladimir Lenin redefined socialism to mean a stage between capitalism and communism. Throughout the early years of the twentieth century, various later stage ideologists used the terminology that was convenient for the manipulation, for the moment and the perpetuation of the movement as they envisioned it.

Because of the need for centralized control of goods and services during World War II in the UK, it was easy to assume the government would be better equipped at managing expanded areas of domestic life. The welfare state of the mid-century United Kingdom was launched by the Liberal Party and led to some important reforms for most of the twentieth century. The effect of almost total state control during the hard years of World War II had resulted in the idea that the state could more efficiently manage problems in vital areas of domestic life. Steve Schifferes, Honorary Research Fellow for the City University of London and a former reporter of economics for the *BBC News*, stated in an article entitled "Britain's long road to the welfare state" that the welfare state of the UK was considered the model to admire around the world. However, throughout the second half of the twentieth century, it declined considerably as an economic model while other European economies outpaced that of Britain.[12]

*Eight*

# WHAT IS A POVERTY MINDSET?

I'm sittin' on the dock of the bay
Watchin' the tide roll away
I'm sittin' on the dock of the bay
Wastin' time...

The Dock of the Bay

--Otis Redding 1967

In her book, *Uncle Sam's Plantation: How Big Government Enslaves America's Poor and What We Can do About It*, Star Parker tells us that her mother learned early on that, "*more than anything else, poverty is a state of mind.*" The author refers to the growing evidence that indicates government dependency strengthens generational poverty and its by-products. I have seen this kind of generational indoctrination transferred so often that those who have bought into the ideology of the welfare state for so long can no longer even imagine a life without government support or handouts. As we say in the UK, they "know their place" as evidenced by the brilliant comedy sketch aired in 1966 on David Frost's *The Frost Report*. The *Class Sketch*, written by Marty Feldman and John Law, delivers a timeless satire of the British class system. At the end of the discourse, when the other two representatives had expressed their supposed advantages, the guy with the shortest stick looks up at the others. He knows that *his place* is at the bottom of the heap. He lacks even a pipe dream of rising above anything. He has no chance, and he knows it.

Children raised in this environment in the UK often see the "free stuff" as their right as to compensation for centuries of classism. Liberal and democratic organizations in the United States continue to claim that racism, sexism, and capitalism are responsible for the problems of the poor on this side of the pond. Star Parker suggests that if there were ever an honest pursuit of viable solutions for the problems of poverty in America, the ubiquitous leftist groups present in policy discussions concerning poverty would be made redundant. She goes on to say that if conservative principles, their traditional values, and the introduction of free markets, were ever implemented and successfully supported, almost all the liberal campaign platforms would vanish.[13]

Parker is aptly describing the failure of Labour governments in the UK to eradicate the problems of poverty for decades as well as the dismal failures of socialistic governments throughout the world. As a young man in the UK, I found it hard to set my sight or even my heart on ambitious goals and to envision achieving a better standard of living for myself and my family. It was a challenge to survive and living from day to day to make ends meet on limited wages and income designated by the state. And then there was always someone nearby who would tell you that you were fighting a losing battle if you thought you could escape from the limited life offered to you by the welfare state. You were supposed to remember your place.

We hear references both in the United States and the United Kingdom about how a poverty mindset impacts violence, poor school performance based on standardized testing, and lower standards of living conditions in impoverished communities. Perhaps a good definition of a poverty mentality is "the mindset that believes one is inferior in quality, inadequate or incapable, a magnet for failure, and lacking in resources. "[14] If one generation passes this mindset to the next, it forms a self-perpetuating foundation for the welfare state or *underclass* that can never be improved or can never see its consistent state of deprivation successfully eliminated. Frustration, wasted talent, and eventually defeat becomes the fruit of this mindset. No one in our culture benefited from dying dreams and faded aspirations. No one will ever do so. The waste of human resources is a tragic and dismal legacy and one from which recovery on all sides is almost impossible.

The expanded version of the welfare state in Great Britain perpetuated the poverty mindset for those who saw themselves as needing to be cared for by the state for life. An institutionalization process can happen on both sides of the prison bars, and this process can be experienced by those who are physically incarcerated or merely mentally handicapped into believing that they could never push past or overcome challenging circumstances.

During my formative years, I was surrounded by the *do just enough* mentality that is so devastating to individual ambition because the only thing that matters is the survival and wealth of the group instead of the individual. This thinking restricted individual accountability and led people to look to someone else to make decisions and choices that should have been personal. The thought was that the stability of a country or people group is dependent on the desired, albeit challenging to obtain, ethical cohesion of the masses. The individual who can make contributions by acting in ways that benefit them personally will eventually be of the most advantageous benefit to themselves and the state as well.

Fair union representation with right and just motives should always be considered an asset to the workers of any organization offering protection against unethical business practices. The general well-being of the people, their prosperity, and the stability of the state in which they live should be the desired goal. The state should serve man, not the other way around. Mankind was never created to serve the state. Rather we should serve the living God, through Jesus Christ in whom all things hold together. Jesus himself said that the Sabbath was designated for man not man for the Sabbath. Similarly, mankind was not created for the benefit of the state. The state was instituted by the people to serve the needs of the people.

> *One Sabbath Jesus was going through the grainfields, and as his disciples walked along, they began to pick some heads of grain. The Pharisees said to him, "Look, why are they doing what is unlawful on the Sabbath?"*
>
> *He answered, "Have you never read what David did when he and his companions were hungry and in need? In the days of Abiathar the high priest, he entered the house of God and*

> *ate the consecrated bread, which is lawful only for priests to eat. And he also gave some to his companions."*
>
> *Then he said to them, "The Sabbath was made for man, not man for the Sabbath. So the Son of Man is Lord even of the Sabbath.*

Mark 2:23-28 NIV

For those of us in the United Kingdom, it was a trap not to be easily avoided since the future, in the grand scheme of things, is always impossible to predict accurately and then adjust accordingly. The future rarely looks exactly like the past. If we think that it always does, then we are setting ourselves and our children up for disastrous disappointment. But we can take note and look for clues. Is it proven somewhere that securing the well-being of the state will benefit the needs of the people? What often seems beneficial for the moment can become a potentially devastating disaster ten years down the road or at least present unnecessary obstacles. It always seems like a good idea at the time.

Fraser Derek, Lecturer in History at the University of Bradford in the United Kingdom states in his book,

> The Evolution of The British Welfare State: A History of Social Policy Since the Industrial Revolution, "The welfare state germinated in the social thought of late Victorian liberalism, reached its infancy in the collectivism of the pre- and post- Great War statism, matured in the universalism of the 1940s and flowered in full bloom in the consensus and affluence of the 1950s and 1960s. By the 1970s it was in decline, like the faded rose of autumn.[15]

A poverty mentality began to seep through the left-leaning communities of the UK like a dense fog common to pockets of the UK during the days of expanded industrialization. Derek continues by revealing that during the 1980s, both the United Kingdom and the United States were seeking monetarist policies that were in direct contradiction to welfare.

Socialistic thought in England diminished individual and inspirational vision in both parents and their offspring. Many parents who taught their children, by example, that they were lucky to have a job. There were very few suggestions or discussions about what you wanted to be when you grew up. You were supposed to grow up and be just like your parents. According to Gosta Esping-Andersen, the United Kingdom system has been classified as a liberal welfare state system. [16] So what were the real and lasting benefits of the welfare states other than assisting people to survive?

Solomon said in his brilliant book from the bible, Ecclesiastes:

*Behold, here is what I have seen to be good and fitting: to eat and drink, and to find enjoyment in all the labor in which he labors under the sun during the few days of his life which God gives him—for this is his allotted reward. Also, every man to whom God has given riches and possessions, He has also given the power and ability to enjoy them and to receive this as his allotted portion and to rejoice in his labor—this is the gift of God to him.*

Ecclesiastes 5: 18-19 AMP.

When we pursue a relationship with God as our Creator and Creator of the world, when we know Him and His ways, it is easy to have faith in Him as having access to all that we will ever need here on earth and as the ultimate provider of those needs. But what is more important is that our self-worth, our value, and self-esteem are all based on what we are to Him for we are His well-beloved. *Beloved, I wish above all things that you may prosper and be in health, even as your soul prospers.* 3 John 1:2 KJV

With this understanding, we now know **who** we are and need no longer compare ourselves to others according to riches or by any standard. For none of the world's treasures, be they material or spiritual are here without His hand. There is nothing that the world has to offer that has not been created by Him. He is the ultimate owner of all things and He watches over all things. *Seek first the kingdom of God and His righteousness and all these things shall be given to you.* Matthew 6: 33 NIV

*For every beast of the forest is Mine,*
*And the cattle on a thousand hills.*
*I know every bird on the mountains,*
*And everything that moves in the field is Mine.*
*If I were hungry, I would not tell you,*
*For the world and all it contains are Mine.*
Psalm 50: 10-12 ESV

*Nine*

# WHAT IS CAPITALISM?

If tomorrow all the things were gone, I'd worked for all my life
And I had to start again with just my children and my wife
I'd thank my lucky stars to be living here today
"Cause the flag still stands for freedom and they can't take that away

And I'm proud to be an American, where at least I know I'm free
And I won't forget the men who died, who gave that right to me
And I'd gladly stand up next to you and defend her still today
Cause there ain't no doubt I love this land! God bless the U.S.A.

God Bless the U.S.A.

-- Lee Greenwood 1984

Nineteenth-century political economists passionately debated the relationship between capitalism and welfare. *The Oxford Dictionary of English* defines capitalism as an economic and political system in which a country's trade and industry are controlled by private owners for profit, rather than by the state. There are varying forms of capitalism to be found throughout the world along with various degrees of free markets and public ownership, and of course, varying degrees of competition, state regulations, and intervention as well as varying capacities of state ownership[17]. The political economist debates of the nineteenth century almost always found common ground about relationship between the market and the state.

Adam Smith, the Scottish economist considered the Father of economics as well as a pioneer theorist of capitalism, referred to the free market as the best way to abolish class, inequality, and privilege in society. He considered state intervention as a hindrance to the process of equalization. He said, "the state upholds class while the (free) market can do away with class distinctions in society." Smith contended in his opus-magnum work *Wealth of Nations*, that division of labour under the umbrella of competition (free market) engenders higher productivity resulting in lower prices and an increase of the standard of living. Strong and healthy markets continue and increase production while impacting pricing and making goods available to many more consumers.

According to an article in *US Economy and News* by Kimberly Amadeo discussing the pros and cons of capitalism, the key takeaways are:

- In capitalism, owners control the factors of production and derive their income from it.
- Capitalism incentivizes people to maximize the amount of money they earn through competition.
- Competition is the driving force of innovation as individuals create ways to do tasks more efficiently.

Amadeo's article informs us that "capitalism requires a free market economy to succeed. It distributes goods and services according to the laws of supply and demand. The law of demand says that when demand increases for a product, price rises. When competitors realize they can make a higher profit, they increase production. The greater supply reduces prices to a level where only the best competitors remain."[18] Competition will inevitably improve the quality of a product if there is a choice. Buyers can choose the product that best suits their tastes. Capitalism should result in the best products for the best prices. This advantage is a notable element that is missing from products produced in a socialistic economy and is one of the things that I noticed about buying goods here in the US. When we came to live in the US, we saw a marked difference in the quality of things that were available for purchase here as compared with the things that I was able to purchase in the UK.

In another study comparing socialism with capitalism by C. Bradley

Thompson, the author cites *laissez-faire capitalism* or the economic system in which transactions between private business parties are free from government intervention, as the only system that aligns with *individualism*. *Individualism* is defined as the habit or principle of being independent and self-reliant; a social theory favoring freedom of action for individuals over collective or state control. *The Oxford Dictionary* defines *collectivism* as the practice or principle of giving a group priority over everyone in it. Thompson lists several forms of collectivistic theory that include socialism, fascism, nazism, welfare-statism, and finally, communism as among its most notable forms.

The author goes on to note the extraordinary level of material prosperity of capitalism throughout several hundred years witnessed by historical record even though few people seem to want to defend capitalism as *morally uplifting*. He points to the current trend of academics, politicians, and the media to denigrate free enterprise systems regardless of capitalism's record of producing prosperous economies. These same intellectuals want to praise socialism while ignoring its record of abject failure. Yet for those who lived through numerous Labour governments in the UK, the reality was that without a free market economy, a prosperous and thriving Great Britain would never have resurfaced. For us, it was like the dawn of a beautiful spring morning heralding long-awaited promises after a long and dismal winter of discontent.

Thompson supports capitalism as the only moral system since it necessitates human beings to interact as "traders-that is as free moral agents trading and selling goods and services founded solely on mutual consent." He refers to the system as a fair one because the criterion for the value of goods to be exchanged is left to the voluntary discretion of the consumer. Therefore, it eliminates coercion by outside parties such as the state.

Success in a capitalistic system should relate to the degree to which one uses his mind, gifts, and talents. He cites honesty, industriousness, insight, prudence, frugality, responsibility, discipline, efficiency, and I would add here diligence as qualities of the individual that eventually produce a good result.[19] These are qualities that my father would heartily support and approve of as markers on the road to success. King Solomon himself would have applauded as he made ample notation of them in his book of Proverbs.

David Cooper, Pastor of Mount Paran Church of God in Atlanta,

Georgia, reminds us that our dreams determine the quality of our lives. He goes on to say that our dreams give us the power to capture and refine our lives and powerfully influence the lives of those around us. Martin Luther King, in his famous discourse *I Have a Dream*, illustrated the importance of a dream as an attainable goal that can make an ethical contribution to the life of an individual as well as to the larger group or society. A dream can vastly improve a people struggling to find justice, truth, and equality for all its citizens no matter how diverse and varied their backgrounds or for that matter, their political perspectives may be. Dr. King communicated the importance of vision.

I noticed a gradual improvement in the quality of vehicles driven in the U.K. with each recent trip back to visit family. I also noticed a difference in the quality of items and clothing in comparison with the lower quality goods that were available in the years after the war. I can only attribute the change to the focus on free-market economic measures that replaced the years of austerity. These changes were introduced by Margaret Thatcher and brought a welcome breath of sunlight to my home during the eighties. I believe that there is still an air of prosperity even now some forty years after her government.

Vision has long been a pre-requisite for the pursuit of quality life and, perhaps more importantly, an indicator of the resulting satisfaction of a life well-lived. King Solomon, noted for exceptional wisdom in directing his subjects in the ninth century BC, believed that where there is no vision, the people perish. Helen Keller said, "The only thing worse than being blind is having sight, but no vision."

Socialistic thought defined by various regimes during recent world history has often restricted individual vision and dreams of self-sufficiency by relegating them as unnecessary and a waste of time. The *collective* dream, in its supposedly, loftier ideology, was considered as vastly more important than the individual. Solomon noted in his famous wise sayings that these kinds of ideas did not contribute to creative potential and personal choice. Without a life dream, there can be no definitive purpose. Without purpose, we begin to question the value of our existence. When we struggle with the understanding of purpose, questioning our worth, our value, who we are, or even why we are, our behavior is negatively impacted. Without a life purpose, we have no foundation or vision to build upon or by which to measure the concept of right and wrong behavior. We resort to doing what is right in our estimation regardless of how we impact those around us.

I recall the President of the National Union of Mine Workers, Arthur Scargill, who organized large groups of mobile strikers that could be conveniently dispatch on short notice. Scargill had been heavily involved in the Communist Party and maintained strong Marxist views that he wanted to introduce into the work climate of the United Kingdom. He expedited the demise of the entire union of mineworkers because of embezzlement and theft of crucial resources. His ambition indicated a complete lack of ethical concern for the workers. His ultimate goal was handsome compensation. In 1993, Scargill participated in one of his archenemies, Margaret Thatcher's Flagship Right to Buy scheme to purchase a property under government allocations for those who have limited resources in the United Kingdom. Even though his plans failed because he was attempting to fraud the government by falsely declaring it to be his primary residence, Scargill had no shame in utilizing Margaret Thatcher's plan to help struggling citizens. Scargill's antics are examples of the potential hypocrisies of some Labour leaders and their self-promoting exploitation of resources while completely failing to protect those who had little voice in the workforce. The strikes lasted so long that workers were unable to feed themselves or their families for weeks as the union leaders persisted in their determination to have control over the businesses. This kind of behavior is the ultimate example of selfishness far from the selflessness listed as a positive quality of socialism.

*Ten*

# SO WHAT'S WRONG WITH SOCIALISM?

But February made me shiver
With every paper I'd deliver
Bad news on the doorstep
I couldn't take one more step
I can't remember if I cried
When I read about his widowed bride
But something touched me deep inside
The day the music died

The Day the Music Died

--Don Mclean 1971

Somewhere in the sixties, the attitude among younger people reflected cynicism, and by the seventies, it displayed itself in full-blown disillusionment exacerbated by the Vietnam War. The music industry on both sides of the Atlantic was delivering hit after hit by aiming blows at traditional values and cultural norms. These norms were poorly modeled and ineptly protected by a generation of leaders who did not always deliver on their promises. The scene was in place on both sides of the pond for social problems and dissatisfaction with traditions. Somebody had dropped the ball.

In the UK, I saw a moral decline among people making poor sometimes, illegal and amoral choices resulting directly from a lack of individual responsibility and accountability. It was easy to play the blame game. *Blame the government* became the popular chant. Those who adhere still manifest this philosophy. The American dissenters began to recite the popular catch phrase. It was reported on the nightly news and caught on even in my corner of the UK. But the chant had a different motive for people who were demanding more welfare-state benefits after years of Labour government ideologies.

Blaming is the most convenient political stance since it relieves individual responsibility, therefore destroying the personal drive. On my side of the pond, it became acceptable behavior to get as much financial benefit as possible from the generous government programs regardless of the instituted restrictions classed as legal pre-requisites. These and other forms of government program abuses began to abound. This kind of mentality was accepted even though people knew clearly that this questionable behavior was wrong. Still, these ideas were passed down and continued by their offspring. It became almost customary to use and abuse such programs that perpetuated forms of cheating the government. It is not surprising that this cycle of generational abuse of government funding intended to temporarily assist the people of a post-wartime economy became even more of a hindrance to a group of people trying to survive.

As a result of the world wars of the first half of the twentieth century, even during the wars, the government became increasingly involved in peoples' lives through a system of rationing of goods, the assistance of employment, and free secondary education. The aftermath of WWI created an economic slump in the country but especially in northern and Midland industrial towns like Warrington, Manchester, Liverpool, and Birmingham. That slump worsened and became the 1930s era Great Depression. The much-needed system of programs came into being because of a demand for reasonable social reform. Unfortunately, the lasting result was an enduring increase in the role of the state and the decline of a free market economy.

The original architects of the government assistance programs were wise enough to foresee problems due to the tendency of group behaviors that would eventually undermine the government as well as the assistance program itself. The early designers of the welfare state programs were careful to ensure that these benefits would be restricted to a *minimum subsistence* level. These restricted benefits were also dependent on given pre-requisites such as length of weeks unemployed, the pursuit of training education in preparation for work, and the number of unemployed during the given period. However, after the victory of the Labor Party in the 1945 general election, the new government eliminated the original precautionary measures so that the people of the United Kingdom could be provided for "from the cradle to the grave."[20]

The Nazi Party in the early stages of its portentous beginnings based its tenets on socialistic ideology mixed with aggressive bullying and physical harassment practices to control dissenters. The Brown Shirts practiced gang-style political *influence* perpetrated on those who did not agree with their ideology. In an uncomfortably similar event that took place in 2018 in Washington, DC, Senator Ted Cruz and his wife found themselves surrounded and confronted by a thug-like gang. The gang would later identify themselves as members of various left-wing organizations and of the Democratic Socialists of America. Groups of this type have even been encouraged by politicians behaving irresponsibly. Maxine Waters, a long-time democratic member of the House of Representatives from California, instructed her supporters to engage in harassment of Cabinet members and supporters of the President of the United States, Donald Trump.[21]

This type of political wrangling and irresponsible behavior from politicians on this side of the Atlantic Ocean is astounding to me. I had admired America for so long from across the Atlantic, and this type of behavior was completely unexpected even inconceivable. This country seemed to me to have always been proud of its provision for the freedom of speech and the ability to vote according to one's consciousness. But perhaps, reality will show that we are beginning to witness somewhat of a pendulum swing set in motion to compensate for past wrongs and failings committed in the name of justice. Perhaps human justice is not, never has been nor ever will be as colorblind or indiscriminate in her decisions as moral responsibility would have desired.

Intimidation tactics demonstrate contempt for any dissenting voice that would challenge the opposing political ideology. It is dangerous to engage, much less promote the idea of shouting down those who do not agree with us. Beware any group that tells you that you do not have the right to voice your opinion. History has clearly shown us that the elimination of freedom by bullying and harassment towards any group leads to disastrous consequences. Perhaps certain American politicians would do well with a refresher course in world history.

I recall a rather harrowing incident in England when I owned and operated a small trucking business that permitted me to transport goods to various destinations in the United Kingdom and provide income for my growing, young family. The incident occurred during a local strike by unionized wire drawers. I needed to transact business with the weights and measures department and weigh in with my truck. During this process, I encountered an aggressive and agitated picket line whose members decided that I posed a threat to their cause and therefore began to verbally and physically threaten me even though I was unarmed and self-employed. One guy left the picket line to throw a punch at me that I was able to avoid thankfully due to my rugby training and agility. I was young and not easily intimidated. I would have defended myself under normal circumstances back then, but due to the aggression and superior numbers of the strikers, I was clearly at a disadvantage. I managed to get back in the cab of the truck and make an escape through the line while strikers hurled insults and missiles.

It is important to note that I have witnessed reports of members of the current American left as well as the extreme right who support the use of this obnoxious form of bullying. This bullying includes shouting down opposition and re-acting violently to any kind of free speech from those who do not agree with their particular ideology. These tactics bare a strange resemblance to the repulsive behavior that eventually resulted in the ultimate power display of bullying in the world's arena, World War II. Just before I was born at the end of the decade of the forties, my family endured this war that was one of the worst wars in human history, and that would significantly influence the politics and direction of the United Kingdom for many years. Was there nothing to learn and take away from this horrific war that might be of use to those who still seek to silence or even eliminate individual business establishments as well as any political opposition today?

In a 2015 article by Martin Robinson for the *Daily Mail* at its online site, a mother of ten children asks the question, "So what if I'm on the dole?" The subject of the article reports that she was being given around

£22,000 a year in handouts and that she wanted her children to follow her example by having five babies each so she can continue to be supported. The television journal program accompanying the report shows her children boasting about how they know the intricacies of the system so they can *milk the system benefits*. Their mother, who has received benefits for thirty or so years, boasts about her use of cash benefits to cover her body with £2000 worth of tattoos and that she buys cigarettes for her children when they help with housework. [22]

In my community, it was not hard to find people with this attitude during the periods of socialistic and Labor governments when work was scarce. Even so, it was still believed by most, that the concept of work, hard work was often the foundation of family stability. Early in the days when the economic assistance began, most felt that once unemployment benefits began, it negatively impacted one's self-respect and dignity. However, the DOLE as the solution to extended joblessness soon became the answer for the main source of income. At the same time as applying for and receiving the DOLE (the Depart of Labor and Employment benefit), more and more people began to feel perfectly justified in taking additional work at small jobs where they received cash wages that were difficult to trace. It was not always the case, but it was hard to find anyone who was actually *on the DOLE* and completely abiding by the government restrictions concerning employment. The common excuse given was that business owners always used technicalities to pay fewer taxes regardless of considering that these lowered taxes quite often permitted the creation of more jobs.

When people found themselves continually in the process of receiving government assistance, they began to justify it and identify the provision as belonging to them as free money. The Welfare State paid DOLE as well as rent for people who did not have a job. It became difficult to ignore that this handout was too generous and began to destroy the incentive to look for employment. This thinking encouraged the mindset of poverty, lowered standards of living, resulting in increases in crime and violence, low motivation to make lifestyle improvements, and for many, eventually gave way to abandoning the pursuit of gainful employment. It was already becoming difficult to find work and then experience the frequent and disheartening disappointment of working for wages that were still insufficient.

An increase of burglaries, frightening home invasions, and continual fraud schemes involving government programs began to be accepted and added to an atmosphere where no one was proud to live. Certain neighborhoods began to be stigmatized by and because of the inhabitants who wanted to live with various forms of abuse of the system.

The system that relies on economic opportunity based on cooperation rather than competition puts its well-being and that of its citizens dangerously at risk since the government of the state and its leaders cannot always be trusted. Such a system also overlooks the fact that people are naturally unlikely to cooperate but more naturally likely to compete. I will never forget the gangs and tribe mentality of the sixties. I know that through all that was around me, I was seeking something more valuable, more lasting, and a life more abundant. I remembered hearing that Jesus came to give life and that more abundantly. I knew that abundant living would come to me and to those that I loved one day.

Socialism, with its strong similarities to communism and its governmentally enforced constraints on the people, is predicated on the idea that individuals will freely and willingly contribute to society based on their ability to do so for the benefit of the common good or ultimately be forced to do so. The tenuous assumption here concerning free will is that individuals would always naturally desire to contribute to society if they can rather than merely profit individually from that society, but that was rarely the case in my community in the UK. The exceptions were those who volunteered to help hospitals by working and shopping at local charity shops. These organizations supported the National Health Service charities and hospices.

A poverty mindset similar in character to a collectivist mindset can manifest as low self-worth of the individual and place the higher value on the group. While this may seem like an admirable human quality, it generally is limited in probability except in utopian societies. Historical reality shows us that most humans have almost always put themselves, their traditions, and most probably the needs of their own family before those of the larger group. The people that I have met through the years that manifest a deeply ingrained poverty mindset, share a collectivist identity, and operate within a strictly socialistic ideology are often the ones who are most angry and who struggle with feelings of helplessness, and low self-worth. They were and still are unwilling to accept that there may be a different side of the story to be considered. They were looking for someone else to hold accountable for the frustration. Blaming someone for the circumstances that they find themselves in developed a habit that soon became a part of their identity. One of my favorite quotes by Oswald Chambers, who is one of my favorite authors, is one with which I can clearly identify. "When I rightly discern what is in me, I cannot despair of any man". Besides Chamber's amazingly insightful observation, I have also seen that placing blame rarely results in contentment of any kind in my life. Rather it hinders my ability to see myself clearly and then prevents me from addressing my own need for improvement. Those who play the blame game cannot accept that happiness and success is greatly impacted by choice. As someone once wisely suggested, "happiness is a journey and not a destination." Oswald Chambers suggested that "Holiness, not happiness is the chief end of man." By constantly pursuing happiness, we miss out on so much. When we become victims of our emotions, we miss what is genuinely good, right, and pertinent in this world and on into the next. From where I stand, there is only one destination worth pursuing and it is firmly and safely encapsulated in the kingdom of heaven.

The faulty concept of satisfaction within limits on our lives proposed by state control is unrealistic and based on an erroneous understanding of human nature. It is a fallacy that the masses will ever be content with limited control of resources as well as extremely limited opportunities for personal growth. Hard work, lots of sacrifices, relatively little gain and little realization of substantial benefits were the expectation in the United Kingdom under Labour government restrictions. It was not a pleasant experience for anyone.

As Star Parker, an American syndicated columnist and author explains, "What should be limited is federal bureaucratic control of our lives." Parker states that individual freedom and personal responsibility have always been necessary and perhaps now more than ever.[23]

What happens when economic ideologies transfer from textbook scenarios into the real and challenging business world? Perhaps one answer is found by examining the free market economies in Pacific countries like Hong Kong, Taiwan, South Korea, Singapore, and Japan. These well-known *Asian tigers* have been prosperous even while lacking natural resources. On the other hand, we have the examples of Russia and Brazil, both rich in resources yet struggling with poverty under socialist regimes that discourage and prevent entrepreneurship. "Bad government policy, not capitalism shoulders the blame for much poverty."[24] I can give good testimony to what bad government produces for its people. I have memories, experiences, and even photographs. I was born and raised throughout the years of various forms of welfare state programs in the United Kingdom.

Socialism in the U.K. evolved into a means to empower a *working-class,* rather than merely assist working citizens. The idea focused on empowerment, and the battle for control has only escalated through the years and reflects similar battles for political power in the United States.

A commonly found socialist definition of a working-class is that this group incorporates the people who must rely on their skills and labour as the sole economic means of living, excluding those who earn income from private business ownership. Generations of British people began identifying themselves as working-class, thus expecting government assistance programs. According to its descriptions and the social hierarchy of the host society, a working-class of people is a group that follows generally, predictable lifestyle patterns that include a shared identity based on certain interests.

I remember that people from my community and social hierarchy seemed to all take vacations at the same time and often in the same place as if this kind of group mentality holidays were the only ones allowed. There was a holiday campground called *Butlin's Holiday Camps* where most people went when they traveled to get a few days away. Later, working-class vacationers began to head for Spain because the weather was hot, and the prices were still low. There was a slight improvement over the quality of the *Butlin's Holiday Camps*, but most English people wanted their vacation resorts to look just like England. One such seaside resort near Malaga, Spain on the Mediterranean Sea was *Lorette del Mar* that specialized in working-class culture familiarities like fish and chips, pubs, and Sunday dinners so that everybody would be comfortable. These tourists from the socialistic working-class culture were not about to leave home even for a vacation. Escaping to Spain was like going from home to home away from home.

These shared interests are contrasted and even pitted against those of people from groups different than themselves. In theory, the members of lower groups of the socioeconomic order and the social hierarchy would often need assistance and sometimes protection from predatory business practices by unscrupulous owners. These business owners are often unwilling because of costs to provide for workplace safety and the well-being of these workers. Problems arose in England when the state began to commandeer these businesses allowing for the benefit of increased power and selfish gain of some labour union leaders instead of only exposing workers to unscrupulous owners. Now the workers faced potential problems on both sides of the fence. These leaders began to exploit and eventually to manipulate those who were originally supposed to be protected by labour organizations. This imbalance of power is reminiscent of the horrific injustices of enslavement or the ghastly justification of death camps.

There is a grave danger for those who may fall victim to ideas such as ethnic cleansing which is genocide for the people who find themselves on the wrong side of this kind of power establishment. The thinking was that the unwelcomed in thought, politics, perspective, and certainly practice must be under control by any means necessary. In Nazi Germany, history revealed there was dangerous zero tolerance for dissension or questions that did not agree with the leading party's ideology. This kind of thinking quickly deteriorated or perhaps eventually exposed its originally conceived interpretation, *you are not like us and, you must be silenced.* The phrase *not like us* echoes memories of the gang and tribal clashes from my years coming of age in the northwest.

This dangerous attitude could go unchecked because the so-called benefits of the nationalistic and fascist majority justified this radical ideology as the answer to all of the culture's problems. Simultaneously and almost in perfect step time, came the marchers of the "Stormtroopers" who were the aggressive force of firepower undergirding Hitler's charismatic seduction of the nation of Germany and the acquisition of confidence of its people during the 1920s and 1930s. Through tactics of bullying and intimidation campaigns, the National Socialist German Workers Party or Nazis introduced the *modern terrifying phenomena* of political violence.

We now understand the basic definition of socialism as an economic system in which the production and redistribution of goods are controlled substantially by the government rather than by private enterprise, which does not include competitive business and economic opportunity and is based on cooperation rather than competition. In theory, the resulting system should have vastly benefited the culture and people who found that they were struggling in times of financial duress. But what ensued through the years of a welfare state in the United Kingdom that produced years of unexpected problems and decline in so many areas, led to the Labour government being replaced in most of the country. Warrington was still an exception. The mindset there was too deeply ingrained.

Margaret Thatcher's enthusiastic response to years of resource depletion and mismanagement in so many areas was literally a breath of fresh air for me. I will share my experiences in several important areas of life in the British Isles.

In the United Kingdom, socialism became "unsustainable" because as Margaret Thatcher reminded, you soon run out of other people's money. When she was elected Prime Minister, the Labour government (socialists) had already run out. The Iron Lady, as she became known was not at all enamored with "government support for inefficient industries, punitive taxation, regulation of the labour market, (and) price controls – everything that interfered with the functioning of the free economy."[25]

During this time, we began to see well-established church buildings become repurposed for entertainment venues. I remember Saint Anne's Anglican Church, my first school site, being turned into a mountain climbing/gym center. As Labour Party leaders became more and more popular, there began to be a rise in atheism and humanism. Irreligion has become increasingly more acceptable under Liberal leaders and Labour Prime Ministers. The present statistics show that non-religious people are the highest ranking in numbers among politicians of the United Kingdom, including the conservative Prime Minister Winston Churchill, a self-declared atheist.[26] Other notable figures from British history that have completely rejected Christian values and beliefs included William Beveridge, considered the "father of the welfare state"[27].

The founder of the NHS, Aneurin (Nye) Bevan, who introduced policies of considerable social reform, was an atheist who studied Marxism before entering British politics and becoming the Minister of Health in 1945. He married an even more left-leaning socialist MP, Jennie Lee (Member of Parliament) with considerable influence on his career and socialistic ideology.[28] Upon close examination, it is obvious that the tie between socialism and the welfare state's divestiture of religious principles continued to negatively influence politics as well as discourage worship in the British Isles through the years after WWII and up to the present.

I remember a ministry project that I participated in during the early sixties. I have fond memories of being a child and working at a Christian youth center on Sunday afternoons. There was a good number of young people coming in from off the streets, and it seemed to me to be doing something worthwhile in reaching out to the community. Later as an adult, I can remember a project for street evangelization in 1991. We were handing out tracts and invitations to our fellowship, the Christian Fellowship. There was a distinct difference in people's attitudes towards God and religion after a long period of socialistic government under Labour party control. There was a complete lack of respect for or even acknowledgment for God. When I came to the US, I was impressed that people were individuals in their attitude and outlook on life and on God. Group mentalities rarely come to the right conclusion about life. In a group, there must be a leader who may or may not voice the desires of everyone in the group. I admired the courage of individuals to express themselves regardless of the group's opinion. Many kept silent because they thought too highly of what others might think and did not want to risk embarrassment if everyone did not agree.

I remember the vacation to Disneyland when the boys were little. The presenters of the show asked for volunteers to come on stage and be part of the show. The only ones who did not raise their hands were me, Barbara, and my children. It took me ages to become comfortable with getting in front of others to call attention to myself. It was after living in America and being an individual in business for myself that I realized if I wanted to keep up in this culture, I would have to adapt. I realized that every man and his dog were potential entrepreneurs who needed to be confident and sell themselves to make an excellent living. We have always envied the Americans for their abilities to stand out and stand up with confidence, especially when they believe in an idea. I understood the powerful potential available to me as an individual. I had finally broken free of the socialist group mentality.

I see this demonstrated in the Ryder Cup Golf Tournament when the

European socialistic group thinking drives the team from Europe while the individual mentality of the Americans keeps them from doing well. Since the Ryder Cup requires the team to work together, the Europeans find it naturally easier because they are used to working in a group. Even so, I am privileged to be able to develop my potential as an individual without having to depend on the group. In the latter case, when the group falls, I will fall.

We should not forget Lenin's words in 1905 and again in 1909 that affirmed Karl Marx's infamous statement, "Religion is opium for the people". He viewed socialism as "incompatible with religious belief: Everyone must be absolutely free to ... be an atheist, which every socialist is as a rule." He wrote that religion was abominable and "that all worship of a divinity is necrophilia."[29] If you are offended by Marx's use of potentially objectionable terminology, you should take note of the history of Lenin's rise to power in the wake of his mentor, Karl Marx's violent ideological tyranny against religion of any kind. Upon his succession, Lenin commenced his murderous campaign perpetrated against thousands to eliminate those who challenged his ideas. This kind of ideology merits at least a glance into the minds and history of the designers who gave birth to the foundational and frightening tenets of the communist, socialist, and democratic socialist ideals that seem to be attempting a resurrection this time in American politics.

Bernie Sanders, candidate for the United States President and his crony, Alexandria Ocasio-Cortez are both members of the Democratic Socialists of America, which claims to be the largest socialist party in the United States. Although not an officially registered party, the DSA is descended from the Socialist Party of America. The DSA's goal is to take over by hijacking the Democratic Party to fulfill its far-left agenda in its overarching mission and ultimate plan to eradicate all forms of capitalism one step at a time.

Perhaps the most disturbing part of this ambitious agenda is portraying this goal as "*in the best interest*" of all its poorly educated and misinformed victims who have undergone indoctrination in the American Education System of today. This group of young Americans is already finding it challenging to maintain strong work ethics because they follow the thinking that they are entitled to all the benefits and little or no sacrifice.

Somewhere they have been misguided in how to take full responsibility for their own lives. How attractive is the idea of *free stuff* that includes education programs, superior healthcare and adequate housing, food, and childcare for everyone? How did we come to the idea that you can get something for nothing? In the UK, we say, "you don't get blood out of a stone".

Capitalism, whether Democratic influenced or Republican influenced, has been the lifeblood of America. In my observations, this mutually binding relationship contributed to the economic success of the nation. In the past, the two leading political parties of American politics were willing to, at least, agree to disagree and find ways to work together for the common good. That is because the same capitalist mindset and work ethics generally have been necessary to both groups with some distinguishing differences according to the implementation and interpretation of the US Constitution since 1776.

The political divide between the two parties of today has never been more pronounced or more dangerous. Perhaps influential politicians like Bernie Sanders and his protégé Alexandria Ocasio-Cortez have been vocal supporters of an extremely far-left agenda producing a great division not only within American politics leading to the elections of 2020 but also within the Democratic Party. The following characteristics which eerily resemble the welfare state programs that undergirded the UK of my younger years will hopefully give a clearer picture of what the US can expect if the DSA ever manages to achieve their goals in the economy and American political landscape.

The DSA, in its mission to re-arrange American politics to fit its extreme liberal agenda:

- Views welfare state programs as a major step in the process of eliminating the capitalistic link between human needs and market scarcity. The Democratic Party has not taken a stance to completely sever all ties to capitalism but rather believes that these welfare programs are ways to improve capitalism.
- Supports the nationalization of hospitals as well as the entire health care system while the Democratic Party stops at believing that the government should provide universal healthcare for all.

- Supports the nationalization of the entire financial sector while the Democratic Party has simply pledged to work towards higher taxation of large companies and corporations.
- Proposes the complete elimination of police patrol and the penal system. On this point, the DSA goes further left than either the American Democratic Party or any of the Labour governments in the UK[30]

In defense of my homeland, I will mention that, thankfully, at no time, even under the most left-leaning Labour governments, was there ever a consideration to completely eradicate the criminal justice system, the police system or the prison system.

In the seventies, I was a spectator at a rugby match between Leeds and Warrington. The two opposing supporters and fans had to be in extreme proximity because of the large crowd. The stadium held about 20,000 spectators that were all crowded at one end of the stadium. Two groups of rival supporters were on either side of the six-foot metal fence that divided the crowd. They were eager to wage their own fierce, tribal battles apart from the game played on the pitch and they had brought plenty of beer bottles to help with the mood of the war. The lone police officer, armed with only his stick and his bobby's hat to try and give the impression of authority among the horde, tried in vain to keep them separated. He might have had more success if someone from the crowd had not thrown a beer bottle at his head. He received a full blast blow and went to the ground. The battle erupted and was fought to the finish. The police tried to intervene, but it was hopeless since there had never been adequate police protection for these kinds of confrontations. The scenario I described was even fiercer among soccer fans. The tribes were known to jump the fences and meet in the middle to battle on the pitch. The soccer players would leave the field to the fans and let them work out their overcharged aggression. The solution was to surround the pitch with thirty-foot-high fences.

One disastrous event was the match at Hillsborough between Liverpool and Nottingham Forest soccer clubs when a surge of fans at the beginning of the game rushed the gate to get in free and crushed the people near the fences. Over ninety spectators were killed. The council of Liverpool decided that the fences needed to be removed and police protection increased. The lack of tribal "cooperation" would always be a problem for the sports fans in the UK even though they could not go any further to the left.

Funding in the Labour government was always inadequate for supplying needed civil services outside of healthcare.

There will be an interesting battle of power over this intriguing debate before the votes are cast in the American presidential election of 2020. We have not even begun to seriously consider the costs of these ambitious programs or the amount of exorbitant taxes that will be required to support them. So far, the leaders of these proposed programs have been unable to determine exactly where the money will come from or even how they plan to obtain said funds. **What they seem to forget is that you soon run out of other people's money.**

While the Democratic Party in America has always leaned towards a more liberal interpretation in the above areas than the Republican conservative ideas of how government should be conducted, the DSA's agenda goes far beyond liberal policies and reaches to far-left ideologies that will radically change the landscape of American politics and of the American economy. For the DSA and perhaps ultimately for the Democratic Party since the former group is more aggressive in its interpretation, capitalism is to be eliminated and should be placed on the chopping block of American politics.

I chose to examine Representative Ocasio-Cortez because of her affiliation with the Green Party through her proposed Green New Deal. The Green Party of the UK conveniently combines environmental and left-wing economic policies and also includes state-regulated public services just as the GND of America does. David Icke, former spokesperson for the Green Party and English conspiracy theorist has made a plethora of ridiculous claims including that a race of reptiles is actually in charge and running the earth.[31] His latest false claims concern coronavirus and his idea that certain mobile phone networks are causing the spread of the virus.[32] Icke also announced that he was a son of the Godhead and predicted the soon devastation of the earth as a result of tidal waves and earthquakes.[33] Even though Icke has been the object of considerable ridicule because of his ideas, his theories that are utterly ridiculous and impossible to prove, have influenced many and caused considerable confusion among those who frequent less reliable news outlets and rely on questionable sources.

Similarly, the marketing strategies, combined ideologies, and economic proposals of the American version of the Green New Deal are questionable and unrealistic. Yet there is a growing popular groundswell of followers in America. David Icke was also somewhat of a household name until his theories were exposed as extremely farcical on a popular talk show in the UK. As of May 1st, 2020, his Facebook page, considered by the company as falling in the category of harmful information, has been removed. YouTube has removed his videos while Twitter and other social media outlets have responded by creating stricter rules in response to Icke's abuse of telecommunications employees and his suggestion of burning down mobile phone towers. Besides, his publishers refuse to publish his books because of his outlandish and damaging claims that there is a group of reptilian leaders who are moving the world towards a New World Order fascist state marking the end of freedom of speech.

The GND, Ocasio-Cortez's version of its British counterpart, proposes regulations and requirements that are "deeply problematic from a liberty standpoint". According to Charles Lehrman, in an article for the *Washington Free Beacon* entitled "Alexandria Ocasio-Cortez's Green New Deal is 'Pretty Much All Fantasy Land'", the objective of the GND seems to focus very little on the environment. Rather its goal is to put into effect leftist economics that will supposedly end poverty while making prosperity, wealth, and economic security available to all its proponents. So far, there have been few if any solutions for the realistic implementation of its radical ideas.[34]

It is my observation and opinion that the buyer should certainly beware when it comes to what I have seen of the Green Party and its affiliates on either side of the pond. Buyers beware indeed!

Someone has said that "capitalism is private ownership of property and socialism is state ownership of human beings. Pick one!!!"

*Eleven*

# THE NATIONAL HEALTHCARE SERVICE

The problem with socialism is that you eventually
run out of other peoples' money.

--Margaret Thatcher

The founding of the National Health Service (NHS) was not originally intended to increase the number of hospitals. It was designed to nationalize the existing system of charitable foundations and municipal provision. The goal was to standardize health care throughout the country, not to increase the availability of care. William Beveridge, a British economist and labour politician, was the author of the 1942 report entitled *Social Insurance and Allied Services* (The Beveridge Report). It would become the basis for the post World War II welfare state. Beveridge believed that there were five *Giant Evils* that included want, disease, ignorance, squalor, and idleness. He also held to the idea that the medical care budget would go down as the health of the general population increased. The standardization and nationalization of health services would prove to have the opposite effect. The system sustained an annual rise in costs because of increasing services and medication as well as an aging albeit healthier population.

On July 5, 1948, the National Healthcare Service came into existence as a result of studies and preparation by the post-war government of Clement Atlee at the Park Hospital in Manchester, the most important city in the working-class north of England that just happens to be only twenty miles from where I was born. In August of 1949, just a year and some days after its inception and while the NHS was still taking its first real steps, I was introduced as the youngest member of my family. The idea of the NHS was generated in the hope of providing good and reliable healthcare to all instead of exclusively to those whose superior financial means would afford this kind of care. The provisions included free treatment to everyone and encompassed even those visiting the United Kingdom. Yet no one could have predicted the extent to which this basic provision of the welfare state would become a continuing and essential principle of government policy in the UK. Even future conservative governments would not be able to reverse certain aspects of the system that was firmly established as a part of the government policy. Yet, with each passing year, we have watched the NHS struggling continually to provide adequate healthcare for the people of the U.K.

Originally, the fundamentals stated that funding would come directly from general taxation and not national insurance. It was understood that the services would benefit everyone, that these services would be free at the point of delivery and that care would be offered according to need instead of the ability to pay.

This brings us to an important reality about the idea that National Health Care in the United Kingdom is free. It was certainly a benefit to its people in varying degrees, but definitely, a benefit that would prove to be anything but free since payment has always come directly from English citizens whether they intend to use the NHS or not. There are currently three sides to the payment for the National Health Service.

First, there is at present, a national insurance payment withheld from any and every wage earner salary each pay period. When the NHS began, this payment was a reasonably affordable expense that paid for all health services. There were no extra fees incurred making it affordable, convenient, and reliable. The British people were happy that this important necessity was provided to them as citizens, but as time went on notable problems requiring changes began to surface. Each change created a deficit that required extra funding. Waiting periods for hospital treatment became extended and more and more inconvenient. In 2018, *The Guardian* reported that the NHS suffered its worst-ever staff and cash crisis and figures revealed an underlying deficit of £4.3 billion.[35]

As of April 11, 2020, the national Insurance payment is 0 percent for the first £183 a week, then 12 percent for the next £962 a week and 12 percent for anything over £1,145. The payment is certainly not small.[36]

At present, according to the BBC news coverage in August 2019, the waiting period or waiting time is currently at three to four months. Waiting time is the time it takes for a patient to receive treatment after being referred to hospital. Currently, there are increasingly long waiting times for important health care needs to be administered. As of August 2020, exactly one year later, there are increasingly long waiting times, and many thousands of people waiting as long as one year with crucial health care concerns.[37] My father, Jack, needed hip replacement surgery at eighty-five years old (in about 1989). He waited about four months before the procedure and endured a great amount of pain until an opening allowed the replacement surgery to take place.

*The Guardian*, in a report from June 2018, stated that the NHS had as many as 107, 743 vacant health service care posts, an increase of 9,268 above the 98,475-total reported three months before. The shortage of nurses at that time was 41,722, equal to 11.8 percent of the entire nursing workforce which causes the NHS to rely on less qualified staff.[38] To address the lack of trained staff, the government offered the nurses bursaries of £8,000 to obtain the necessary training and degrees. The plan was ineffective because the newly qualified nurses left their old positions for better-paying jobs and left the previous positions unfilled.

In a more recent report as of March 2020, Boris Johnson stated the current figure to be closer to 50,000 nurses short. Siva Anandaciva, chief analyst at *The King's Fund* think tank, said, "After a punishing summer of heatwaves and ever-increasing demands on services, today's report of massive understaffing shows that the NHS [was] headed for another tough winter…In an illustration of the NHS's ongoing parlous financial situation, the Barking, Havering, and Redbridge NHS acute trust in north-east London had to ask the Department of Health and Social Care if it can borrow about £100 million to help is through 2018-2019." [39]

Similarly, there is a shortage of at least 40,000 National Health Care physicians particularly in the Midlands and East of England. On February 16, 2019 issue of *The Guardian,* the Health policy editor, Denis Campbell reports on the record numbers of NHS staff resigning because of poor work-life balance noting unprecedented numbers of employees leaving, many of them citing long working hours as one of the reasons for quitting, has increased 178 percent since 2011[40]. It is worth noting also that the shortages are there partly because doctors can earn a considerable amount of increased salary outside of the NHS at private healthcare practices and in other countries due to certain tax policies aimed at exploiting wealthier taxpayers. This situation has influenced specialized physicians and surgeons to exit the workforce much earlier than normal. The report reveals the problem of progressive taxation and the harm inflicted on patients in the UK. Since 2013, 585 surgical practices have closed their doors leaving 1.9 million patients without care. Ben Johnson, in his article for Foundation for Economic Education, entitled *"Why the UK Suddenly Is Suffering from a Physician Shortage"* from June 2019 says, "The NHS is in a state of perpetual crisis characterized by doctor shortages, long wait times, and rationing. The UK lost 441 general practitioners last year and had 11,578 unfilled vacancies."[41]

In September 2019, according to *The Kings Fund,* the government of the United Kingdom announced increases to budgets for capital investment, public health and the education and training of the workforce, yet these increases were slated to rise only by 2.9 percent from 2019 through 2021. "While the NHS funding deal will ease current pressures, it is not enough to simultaneously restore performance against key waiting times standards and transform services to deliver better care."[42]

Analysis of NHS staffing profiles and trends confirm the previous reports of continued deterioration for certain important staff groups. The NHS is now starting to offer a supplemental service to compensate for shortages in the system. This update requires funding that necessitates a new and separate payment apart from the insurance currently being withheld from wages. To maintain the standards, wage deductions are also continuing to increase while taxation is multiplying. The political party that supports socialistic ideology continues to vigorously promote the NHS. In every election campaign, these same candidates promise much-needed funding for the NHS but when they are elected, their only solution is to raise taxes even further to realize this funding.

Secondly, due to these increased taxes required from citizens to compensate for quality deficits that occurred with the rising costs of services and medication, it became quickly evident that maintaining important standards in health care quality for these services would require considerable extra funding. Who will bear the costs of maintaining such standards that were for the benefit of the people? The answer is evident. Again, the people would have to endure increased taxes in addition to paying four to five times more than the original manageable percentage dedicated to the NHS from wages. These continual tax hikes perpetrated on wealthier British citizens have shown to be harmful in that they reduce the supply of medical providers, temporarily leave patients without a trained physician, and close down small shops while benefiting bigger businesses that absorb the smaller ones. These tax hikes also result in favoring wealthy patients due to consolidation in high-population areas since the higher number of clients is sufficient to support them and often increases travel time and costs for rural and poorer patients. These patients may need to rely on public transportation. Doctors are discouraged from choosing to specialize and use their skills because of taxation and overregulation.[43] In summation, the standards of National Healthcare Services may not be able to keep pace with the needs of the nation. A crisis such as the one presented by the COVID-19 outbreak could have easily overwhelmed the system. Thankfully, the citizens of the United Kingdom have played an enormous role in sustaining the overtaxed system. There have been an estimated 400,000 volunteers who have offered a hand to reduce the strain on the medical staff that was already struggling to keep pace with the nation's requirements during normal circumstances.

Thirdly, charitable organizations are essential to assist in the management of the huge financial burden of maintaining hospitals, physician's salaries, and increasingly, expensive health services. There are currently large numbers of charitable organizations that seek to assist their proponents. It is customary to make contributions and donations of secondhand goods as a gesture of good citizenship to help.

At the time of publication of this book in 2020, the world and the United Kingdom are experiencing the pandemic crisis and its aftermath due to the Coronavirus. We have yet to determine the consequences of an already strained healthcare system in the U.K. What will that mean for the future of a system struggling for years with sky-rocketing costs and medical staff shortages? We can only hope that the system will not continue to be overwhelmed. Perhaps whatever the outcome will be, improvements for the future of the NHS will be an important legacy of the COVID-19 pandemic.

When I first came to the United States some twenty years ago, American friends and acquaintances would challenge and question the performance and quality of the National Healthcare Service in the United Kingdom. I would respond with fervent support of the NHS since I was born into the National Healthcare Service system, but on review, I remember experiencing several problems over the years. It was the only healthcare system to that I had ever known. However, looking back at my childhood visits to the infirmary, I recall a rather serious leg injury resulting in a two-inch long gash. At the time, I was only given one stitch for the deep gash due to efforts to control medical costs incurred by the infirmary. The evidence of the laceration, having never been properly stitched, is still on my leg.

When I was ten, I went to the dentist to have a filing. The dentist decided that he wanted to save the Novocain for more painfully, ailing patients. He proceeded to fill my tooth without the pain relief, which almost rendered me unconscious. The good dentist never even apologized but continued drilling. As you can imagine, to this day, I have a strong dislike for dentist visits.

At the age of seventeen, while playing in a rugby match, I was pushed into a wall, breaking my arm above the elbow and causing excruciating pain. After being in a cast for seventeen weeks, the x-rays showed that it had not been set correctly at the outset. The scans showed a considerable gap in the alignment. After fifty years, I can still feel the pain on a wet or wintry day.

Rationing of health care procedures seemed to become an accepted routine. My father needed a hip replacement procedure at eighty years old. He was in considerable pain but managed with his usual good spirits to wait out the four months before he could receive the operation. *Non-urgent* operations are pushed back for weeks and months with long waiting lists commonplace in the publicly funded National Healthcare Service.

We all thought of it as normal. It was only after coming to America that I realized how abnormal and inhumane some of the treatment was. I can chuckle a bit when I remember my own experiences. My mother's hospital days are more painful to recall, but the reality is that this problem will continue or even become worse for many if there is not enough funding for the system. I shudder to think about a similarly, poorly funded system in a country of more than 330 million people such as the United States and what it will mean for the future of this country as medical costs continue to rise.

When my mother was diagnosed with kidney problems in the late sixties, she was admitted to hospital and assigned to a bed in a large ward with several patients who were sick with various serious ailments. She had only curtains for separation and privacy from the other patients. During one of my visits with my mother, she was distraught and complained about not being able to sleep because of the constant noise from other patients and medical staff. The most overwhelming condition for me to see her in and for her to endure was the constant lack of hygiene. The resulting odors from unattended bodily fluids, even having to view unsightly excrement on the ward floors often left unattended because of the insufficient number of servicing staff and high number of assigned patients were almost too much to bear. My father managed to pay for private care that enabled her to leave the ward in the hopes of better circumstances. However, my mother was never released from hospital services under the NHS and passed in her sleep about three weeks after admittance.

After we immigrated to the United States in 1998, when Barbara had the frightening incident after falling unconscious while working one day, she immediately underwent a series of tests due to an undiagnosed heart condition. We soon understood that her condition was serious. As I mentioned earlier, I was immediately thankful that we were in the United States and that she would receive prompt care without the usual waiting periods. There was a notable difference between her hospital stay in Warrington Borough General Hospital where she underwent a hysterectomy before we left the U.K. Barbara was assigned a bed in Warrington, in a ward with several other people. The NHS was still assigning multiple patients to a ward, as was the case during the early days of the health system. Instead of private and semi-private rooms such as those found in American hospitals at this time, Barbara had to share a large room with strangers. There was almost no difference in the kind of hospital stay that my mother had experienced in the sixties. I understood the reason why paying for additional health insurance carried certain benefits. Americans preferred to pay private insurance when they could afford it, which allowed for the best conditions and treatment possible.

The payments assigned to the National Healthcare Service that are a part of every wage earners salary deduction do not provide for this kind of private treatment in hospital. You must pay extra and above the required amount that is a part of the National Insurance payment. The National Insurance payment is never adequate to provide necessary hospital services. The program is supported by volunteer charities designated for each hospital.

Barbara's heart condition would cause a repeated attack here in the United States about a year later that ultimately cost her life. Upon reflection, I was thankful for the last year that we had to spend together. I believe it to be because the care she received here in the United States without having to wait for treatment.

Over the twenty-years that I have lived in the United States, I have continued to receive more negative reports from friends and family members back in the UK about the performance, increased waiting periods, and continually deteriorating lack of quality of service for the NHS. It is still difficult for them to relay such unfavorable reports since we all have nationalistic pride for our homeland. Even though it is hard to admit, there have been many questionable experiences. It was not at all surprising to hear of and read about the 40,000 physician shortage and 50,000 nurse shortage due to the lack of funding.

More recently, my American wife, who worked for an airline as a flight attendant, was on a layover in the London area. She began to feel ill and realized that she had run out of and forgotten to pack extra medication for Diabetes Mellitus. She called me, and I immediately sent her in a cab to the nearest hospital in Brighton where she was laying over. At the hospital, she was given extra medication that would last her until returning to the US. She was immensely grateful and reported to me upon returning home that the staff was extremely kind, "having looked at me puzzlingly when I tried to pay for the service." Even though we were grateful for the assistance, we later talked about the high costs of a system that would so generously respond to every foreign patient who found him or herself in need of medical care. However, at the time, my American wife was shocked at the appearance of the hospital and said that it looked like something out of a 1940s movie with barely visible lighting from dim bulbs and gray corridors.

We have a younger American friend who married a British man, moved to the London area, and had her first child there in hospital. She was, of course, placed in a ward where she could hear all the procedures and smell every bodily function produced by her nearby ward mates. She also talked about the outdated facilities in which the nurses and doctors managed to do a fantastic job. Even though she always had great respect for her new home and friends, and very much appreciated the thorough mid-wife care and her constant, timely visits, she decided to have the second child in private care.

In the 1980s, to assist citizens with health care services, Margaret Thatcher's conservative government promoted the use of the private medical system, British United Provident Association BUPA established in 1947. This program was designed to provide additional healthcare and to alleviate the pressure on the NHS by allowing individuals to purchase private care. BUPA private health programs differ radically from the NHS tax-funded health care system. Quality of services, waiting periods, private hospital beds, and modernized facilities are offered to its patients. According to recent statistics, BUPA is now an international health care group serving around 32 million customers in 190 countries at the time of publication supplying premium services and medical providers.

As of 2019, its revenue at the half-year point was 6.0 pounds sterling.[44] Because the socialized system was inadequate, the addition of private healthcare companies has proved to be essential to offering quality healthcare services in the U.K. In fact, it seems that many Europeans in all countries want to seek private healthcare for reasons such as a second medical opinion, the avoidance of extreme waiting periods and the avoidance of risks from infections in public facilities.

One of the essential issues in each election campaign in the country is still the discussion of how each party will fund the NHS. "There is no free lunch." Margaret Thatcher said, "Socialism cannot sustain itself because it runs out of other people's money." Who was going to pay? Conversations began about sustainability even among those who lived moderate lifestyles. Health services relied on contributions from their wealthier fellow citizens in the form of taxes. People began to use their wits to devise better ways to collect even more "benefits" from a struggling economy and overburdening taxation of all citizens. They began to say, "Let someone else pay for your life. You do not have to work. You do not have to save. You do not even have to think for yourself. Let the government do it for you." The reality of the situation was and still is that someone had to sustain and pay for this *paradise.*

What is the current status of the National Healthcare System today and how well does it function in surviving the rising costs to address the growing needs of its benefactors? On October 31, 2019, *The Times* reported that Matt Hancock who is currently the health secretary stated that the NHS is an essential issue and top priority. The current concern is that the available funds are insufficient to meet the demand. While hospitals continue to miss their targets, there are 4.4 million people on waiting lists for operations. Hospitals are being used more and more each year as the aging and number of sicknesses they face yearly increases with no relief in sight to stem the tide. [45] The *Daily Mail* reported in early December of 2019 that more than 320,000 people waited longer than four hours in emergency rooms while the performance record in general for the NHS waiting times has been the worst on record in 2019. The author gives evidence that figures are showing that the NHS is not just facing crises in the winter months while recovering in summer but instead is "under immense strain all year round." Doctors have warned the country's emergency care is imploding. [46] Britain's leading General Practitioner, Helen Stokes-Lampard, reported to the *Daily Mail* in late October of 2019 that it takes seventeen minutes to switch on her outdated NHS computer. The NHS scrambles to find technology improvement solutions for its growing, aging population. Professor Stokes-Lampard is a top physician and the Chairman of the Royal College of GP's, the largest Medical Royal College in the UK. She stated that the computer system at her practice in Staffordshire is over a decade old and that she can hardly "get through a morning" of seeing patients without it crashing.[47]

Perhaps the most daunting challenge that the NHS has had to date has hit the shores of the United Kingdom in the form of the global COVID-19 pandemic. Because of years of existing budget crises and enormous shortages of health care workers, there is concern that the strain to an already overtaxed system could be irreparable.

*Twelve*

# UNION POWER

Gis a job

*--Jimmy* "Yosser" Hughes

Yosser was one of the main characters from Alan Bleasdale's 1982 television series *Boys from the Black Stuff* played by Bernard Hill and set in Liverpool during the late seventies and early eighties. In those days, Liverpool was undergoing high unemployment and increasing crime. Many were unemployed as the large employers of the coal mines and car manufacturers shut down the business and ended production. Yosser's tragedy stemmed from his mental instability and his lack of a job. It made it impossible for him to provide for his children. The catchphrase *Gis a job* summed up the feeling of desperation commonly experienced in the early eighties.

During my early working days, I remember a union leader who headed the union in a local company. This labor leader struck terror in the hearts of upper management officials because of his ability to lead the unions. At the mere mention of the word *strike*, he secured each demand on his list. Eventually, the company had to capitulate. It sent its product to be handled by another company to be able to produce a profit. Soon afterward, the company closed its doors. Hundreds of people became unemployed yet again because of the unrealistic demands of labor union bosses.

After Joe H. went into business for himself, he began paying exorbitant taxes. He then realized that a socialist government was not consistently beneficial for enterprise. Nevertheless, enterprises provided jobs. Jack S went to work in Liverpool as a staunch socialist and changed his views radically after working there for only six months because of his work as the district manager of an insurance business required that he visit clients. He learned that they were taking advantage of the government in every way possible rather than finding reasonable employment to take care of themselves and their families. Instead, they came up with schemes to commit fraud against the very government that was working to alleviate their problems. Not only did we see an increase in the number of burglaries and frightening home invasions, but there were also more incidences of social security fraud.

A recent article from the paper the *Liverpool Echo* reports that Liverpool is "on the edge of the abyss" again. The pandemic of 2020 has instigated what the author referrers to as a "perfect storm" scenario forcing the town council to consider filing an emergency order imposing a ban on all spending above the necessary services. Even with the ban, that notice might not be sufficient to aid the city in crisis. Due to austerity measures in the UK, the city council has lost 430 million of its funding in addition to its overburdened budget that was already dangerously short on reserve funds. With the arrival of the Coronavirus pandemic, it became evident that the challenge would be daunting for areas of high-level poverty and poor health. Liverpool has consistently been among the cities that fit that description. The city's limited resources coupled with high rates of health issues, homelessness as well as the loss of essential revenue from city-run venues like leisure centers and car parks. Considering the UK's austerity agenda, the Liverpool government has been told only to rely on business rates for its income. However, Liverpool is a city firmly entrenched in socialistic ideology with leftist principles since the middle of the twentieth century. There would be few who have sufficient ideas on how to encourage businesses to produce badly needed capital for their local government and maybe even fewer who have the desire to do so. Unfortunately, thousands of businesses in this struggling city have recently closed their doors, possibly for good. Government funding in the UK is not allocated based on deprivation and need, which would be a reasonable expectation for a socialistically run council. The government of the UK has now allocated funding per capita, leaving Liverpool with an enormous deficit of about £44 million. [48]

Since reasonable choices and options for life work and goal-oriented ambitions were few in our working class, socialistic environment. Even though early in my young working life, there seemed to be plenty of work. The available factory jobs began to disappear as industrialization would eventually give way to a "free market economy" to maintain a viable way of life for all people in the United Kingdom.

In the battle between conservative and extreme left labor unionization, the representatives of the leftist groups could not allow their debating opponents to speak or even get a word in as if they were afraid of being wrong. This situation brings to my mind a political debate televised in the eighties between a socialist and conservative Member of Parliament. After minutes of frustrating exchanges due to the Labour representative's inability to allow a fair discussion because of his bullying tactics and constant interruptions, the conservative member finally responded by saying. *Anyone who won't let his challenger speak must be completely on the defensive and insecure about what he is trying to communicate.* The baffled Labour party member went quiet.

Several leaders of the 1980's Labour party challenge to Margaret Thatcher's Conservative government were well known for using strong rhetoric and acerbic wit. Dennis Skinner, who was one of the most passionate challengers, was among this group of dissenters in Parliament. I remember him to be an extremely far-left socialist leader whose ideology was very borderline communism. He did not hesitate to interrupt those whom he felt were in opposition to his left-leaning ideas. I also remember viewing the television newscasts of the Parliament session where he was among those attempting to corner Margaret Thatcher regarding the creation of wealth and opportunity. Her masterful leadership style is worth viewing. You can find her brilliant and entertaining dialogue on the perils of socialism for the UK on YouTube's *"Thatcher's Last Stand against Socialism."* For many British conservatives, Thatcher was considered the most effective and influential Prime Minister of the last century. Her fruitful and productive coalition with Ronald Reagan in the eighties was inspirational. Any female considering launching a successful campaign for the American Presidency would do well to take a page from the Iron Lady's playbook. We are blessed to have a Margaret Thatcher only once in a lifetime. It will be a long while before we see another one.

After a six-year apprenticeship as a workshop engineer specializing in tool making, I decided that I would not be satisfied with the limited growth opportunities. I saw the workers as well as managers trying to evade work in any way they could. I remember that I was in a workshop with people that were only a few years from retirement. I have heard that statistics indicate that people who may have worked for a lifetime don't always survive in retirement for long. Accordingly, several of those who had already retired from the company died within a few months. Many of them had little or no positive outlook on life, no specific purpose, nothing to do, and no outlet for personal self-expression because they were inclined to think of themselves as part of a group. They could only exist as part of the group.

I have always wanted to work, making my living and be as independent as possible owing little to anyone, since being a young lad. Perhaps I learned more than I realized from watching my parents work hard. Similarly, I have never had the desire to retire and certainly not retire early. I remember so many people who retired and died within a couple of years after leaving their posts. Without a purpose and without finding an enjoyable and meaningful job, and especially finding yourself alone after being and thinking as a group for such a long time, it becomes easy to lose interest in life.

George Burns reminded us in the movie *The Sunshine Boys* that "The happiest people I know are the ones who are still working. The saddest ones are the people who retire."

Two of my friends, Les G and John K, joined me in a small business venture in 1978. We started a Fishing Pond Club as a recreational outlet for people in the area. My partners were always in opposition to my conservative business ideas. I was in the minority when they were determined to run the business on socialistic ideals. Instead of first creating our customers, they wanted to try to refurbish and perfect the venue. There was not enough capital. We soon ran out of cash before we could get our wings for taking off even though it was a "capital" idea to have a pond where people could fish and enjoy being outdoors. I remember realizing quite well that Margaret Thatcher's ideas were worth our attention.

The work environment in the factories was in no way conducive to personal ambition. To be promoted, someone had to die. You had to fall into a dead man's shoes before there was an opening. Even if a position opened, you had to compete for the post or be a favorite of someone with influence. I began preparing to leave the apprenticeship, and find greener pastures, more opportunities and outlets more suitable to my growth and development. My fellow workers, particularly the older, more experienced ones with whom I labored from day to day, were extremely discouraging. They tried to convince me that I would never make it on the outside of the engineering factory. It felt like I was trying to leave prison for the free world after years of institutionalization. I wanted something more, much more. Now when I go back, the differences are quite noticeable between the mindsets of my friends in the UK and the bustle of activity that is still available to me in these later years of my life. I still have the freedom even now and can enjoy new pastimes with enthusiasm. I can have enjoyable experiences with people in my age group as well as those from a variety of younger age ones. Among my peers there in the UK, it seems that the same kinds of limitations that I was eager to escape when I left for a future with more choices are still present. Even if it is only a mindset left over from years of Labour government restrictions that hinders creativity, productivity, and excitement, it was a handicap. It's almost as if an invisible fence that separated us from the shiny, American vehicles, has still yet to be torn down. I am thankful for the changes to the British way of life and my life as a young adult that were introduced during the days of Margaret Thatcher. It was said of the Iron Lady, "Thatcher Can Do!" This statement alone was in complete opposition to the socialist rhetoric that seemed like brainwashing that restricted by limitation. The socialist statement said, "You can only do what you're doing. Keep mining, laboring in the steel mills, or cutting wire in the wire industry." For the workers, it was back to the dismal and discouraging propaganda meant to keep the dreamers in place.

During my apprenticeship, my wife, Barbara, was expecting our first child. It meant that we could not depend on her salary as a supplement to my income at the time. My salary of twenty pounds a week in 1970 would barely cover our expenses. I even worked overtime on Saturdays and Sundays. I seemed to be working harder but not making any real progress for me or my family. I had to seek help from my father, who moved in with us, which made it even harder for me to stand on my own and to pursue my dreams.

Also, I began to become even more frustrated because of the frequency and number of strikes and their significant impact on my earnings. I knew that I was making the correct decision for us. I earned a raise of ten pounds during the first week of my employment in the life insurance business as opposed to my factory job, and I knew that I could work towards a desirable goal for the future.

I remember the bread shortages due to strikes and picketing. In 1976, I owned a small shop that resembled a neighborhood grocery store. I had to ration my customer's bread purchases caused by shortages. Bread was in limited supply thanks to the abruption of out of control labor strikes and the continual demand for food by the growing number of consumers. None of my customers were satisfied, and some were furious, as I tried to provide for my regular customers, creating constant headaches for me in a business that required that balance of supply and demand.

Also, in 1976, I owned my own small goods trucking business. I attempted to deliver an urgent shipment for one of my customers due to be shipped from the docks in Liverpool. The line of traffic to access the loading bay was over a mile long, which would delay the shipment by at least one or two days. I decided to go past the waiting vehicles in the strike line and do the small unloading job by myself. The striking dockworkers were so angry at my actions that it became clear that it was exposing me to a violent exchange. I quickly unloaded my shipment and thankfully got away without a confrontation. Forceful union leaders demanded that workers strike at the drop of a hat and for the smallest reason. Some reasons were utterly ridiculous such as the morning toast was late, or there was no butter. Not long after, this same dock was closed due to a proliferation of constant strikes and the resulting late deliveries.

In a page taken from the British newspaper *The Sun* from January 11, 1979, you will find an article entitled "Crisis? What Crisis?" which describes the reaction of the tanned Prime Minister Jim Callaghan upon returning from holiday to find the state of the railway, trucking industry, and jobs in general in complete chaos as a result of Labour government mismanagements. Callaghan's inept leadership made the Thatcher government a welcomed change.[49]

Rubbish piled up outside of Royal Shrewsbury Hospital in 1979

Courtesy of The Shropshire Star

https://www.shropshirestar.com/resizer/g4Yy4n__t3Adf3meN4aV k5MHX4Q=/990x0/filters:quality(100)/arc-anglerfish-arc2-prod-shrop shirestar-mna.s3.amazonaws.com/public/NOY5MOPOF5F6PO4F3 TUAW5B4KY.jpg

In an article in January 2019 from *The Shropshire Star*, the author describes "Misery Monday" as the largest disruption of civil services since 1926. The rest of the week was equally dismal and included food shortages for seriously ill hospital patients. At the same time, lines of angry truck drivers who were protesting against a strike on the M6 highway, an important circulation route in the north of England, formed a convoy. Unions warned of frightening consequences if there were any attempts to make travel on the roads safer by gritting the dangerous roads.[50]

I had two very, close friends who were both strong supporters of the Labor government until they went into business for themselves. They soon began to discover that running a successful business required them to pay close attention to hiring, taxes, and wage payments. They realized the benefits of lower tax rates for their businesses to continue to provide jobs for their employees. One of them changed his politics after living and conducting business in Liverpool and having to face exorbitant taxation. Yet the second of them was still unwilling to reconsider his socialistically based opinions because of training ingrained from being born and raised in the cultural mindset of the Labour party in the north of England. He was unwilling, almost seemingly unable to make the transition as if the mental conditioning had been too potent. The recent national elections in 2019 produced a landslide victory for the conservative party. In the United Kingdom, the color red represents the Labour party, while the color blue indicates a Conservative area on the map. It is the exact opposite of the political landscape map in the United States. The UK map of voters has always been overwhelmingly red (representing leftist policies in the United Kingdom) in the Merseyside area that centers on the city of Liverpool and its surrounding boroughs. In the 1980s, Liverpool found itself on the verge of bankruptcy because the Labour party government was not only slow at providing jobs but also short on productivity because of union restrictions and constant strikes by workers. These inadequacies meant that there was no income to be taxed. The scenario was a classic socialistic disaster.

Margaret Thatcher informed the Mersey Militants and supporters of the Liverpool Labour Party that there would be significant cuts. In 1983, Mrs. Thatcher won a second general election by a landslide while the Labour Party won the Liverpool city council elections by promoting a radical socialist manifesto. Even so, not all of Liverpool was in support of the socialist manifesto, and the city found itself financially strapped as well as divided. Soon the Labour councilors were banned from public office.[51] Yet again, even after thirty or so years, the argument for decentralization is being reprised.

In Great Britain, the more government involvement in the lives of the people, the less individual control over the major life choices they actually had, and the greater the potential for corruption by all involved parties even though the original intentions were instituted for the common good. Without changes allowing for movement in a free market economy, this system of powerful government control was doomed to failure in keeping with the words of Margaret Thatcher: "You will soon run out of other people's money."

*Thirteen*

# TAXATION

Let me tell you how it will be
There's one for you, nineteen for me.
Cause I'm the taxman, yeah, I'm the taxman

Should five percent appear too small
Be thankful I don't take it all.
Cause I'm the taxman, yeah, I'm the taxman

Cause I'm the taxman, yeah, I'm the taxman
And you're working for no one but me.

The Taxman

--George Harrison *1966*

George Harrison brilliantly summed up the conditions of heavy taxation under the Labour Government in 1966. At the same time and with the same concerns, the Rolling Stones took up residence in France to avoid outrageous taxes in the UK. Even though taxation was also high in France, they were far less than the rate in Great Britain.

For as long as I can remember, everything in the United Kingdom was taxed to the hilt, and high taxes continue to be the norm still even now. Even when the conservatives are in government, taxes remain high because taxpayers have long since adjusted to the high rates of taxation.

In 1980, I owned a small grocery store. The cost of a bottle of whiskey was ten pounds. Because of extortionate tax rates along with another tax category, the Value Added Tax (VAT), my profit on this one bottle was only ten pence (ten cents). This brand of liquor was so popular that I had to keep it in inventory without being able to make a profit because demand was so high.

Taxes were always a major concern for the shop owner whose profits are directly impacted. Over the years, the taxes on a gallon of petrol (gasoline is sold in the UK by the liter since it is normally so expensive) have steadily increased. Due to the tax rate last year on our last visit to the UK, gasoline costs were approximately six US dollars per gallon. All of this is simultaneously taxed along with all other taxable items. There is rarely any reduction in tax rates, even when the conservative government is back in power because people have already gotten used to paying the higher rate.

In a report by Nick Sorrentino in 2013, the author talks about living in the United Kingdom as a small child.

> When I was a small child, we lived in the United Kingdom for a couple of years just before the Thatcher revolution. In the years afterward, after we were back in the states and I was a bit older, I could remember my parents talking about how colossally messed-up Britain was economically. The 1970's weren't great for America but for our friends cross the pond, they were far worse.

> My parents would talk about 'brownouts' when the electrical workers would deliberately turn off the power from power plants in a show of what some might call 'workers solidarity'." Sorrentino goes on to talk about his experiences in a later article about Margaret Thatcher in 2018. "In the years after World War II, socialism, real hardcore, *state owns means of production* socialism, swept into the UK and it failed in a miserable disgusting mess. Britain, which had once shined, which was once a 'nation of shopkeepers' (I [author] have always loved this characterization), was relegated to a damp and dreary shadow of its former self.

The whole place had the smell of mold and economic stagnation. Then, finally, Margaret Thatcher introduced a ray of light that provided hope.

Sorrentino's mother told him of the time she almost lost her life in a British hospital. She was experiencing an ectopic pregnancy. Instead of treating her, the doctor sent her home, suggesting that the problem was most likely indigestion. Twenty-four hours later, she was undergoing surgery in the Naval Hospital. To recover after surgery, she was put into a room full of other people and had to endure screams of anguish not to mention conditions difficult to bear because of a lack of privacy. His mother's words were, "Never go into a European hospital if it can be avoided." Sorrentino claims to have learned early on that socialism was not the way to go.

For the Sorrentino family, the incredible levels of taxation in the UK were a constant topic. He writes,

> As my father was an officer in the US Navy, he did not feel the burden but I can remember him talking for years about the audacity of a government that thought it had the right to take nearly 100% of people's pay.
>
> My dad explained that one of the reasons all the cool British bands of the sixties, left the UK and came to the United States was because of the rate of taxation in the Isles. This is an amazing thing given that the rates weren't exactly low in the US either. At least Uncle Sam didn't take everything.[52]
>
> This level of taxation was the inspiration for a memorable Beatles tune.

The pain was brilliantly lamented in George Harrison's 1966 hit song *TaxMan*.

> Let me tell you how it will be,
> That is one for you nineteen for me.
> Should 5% appear too small?
> Be thankful I do not take it all.

After the song was written, the record shows that the UK felt that a 95 percent tax rate was not enough and boosted it to an extra 3 percent. This action on the part of labor government leaders at the time reveals an example of pettiness by a government that "gave the knife a little extra push just because it could."[53]

The rate for British taxpayers reached 83 percent in the mid-1960s. The wealthiest among them paid a 15 percent super tax on top of that continuing to push taxes as high as 98 percent. [54]My first wage packet in 1965 was £2.86 out of which I was able to pay reasonable rent and board.

When taxes continued to be sky-high during the seventies, many entrepreneurs became disheartened and began to find ways to avoid reporting their full revenues because of burdensome taxation. Offshore bank accounts became normal practice. Top entertainers like the Rolling Stones went to live in France since the French rate of taxation was still considerably lower than that of the UK.

I recall many times working a long shift on a Saturday earning one and a half times pay or a Sunday earning twice the hourly pay. The utter disappointment was unforgettable when my workmates and I received our paychecks and saw the crippling income tax deduction. We all agreed that it wasn't worth doing the overtime. All incentive to excel, work harder, and perform at a higher standard disappeared, and our spirits were crushed.

Studies show that an economy with progressive rates of taxation or high taxation can cause handicaps to the creation of businesses that then create jobs. It stands to reason that entrepreneurs, who may desire to set up businesses, would likely be discouraged by governments that demand a high percentage of profits. They would often prefer to work abroad, which is exactly what I decided by bringing my small business and several business ideas to the United States. It was due to unreasonable taxation that I was forced to close the business that I had left in the United Kingdom. Extreme taxation can have a damaging effect on an economy and then still fail to sufficiently increase tax revenues.

The current high rate of taxation presents problems for many. My sons and their families are living with burdensome tax rates even at the time of publication. One of them has found it more financially advantageous to leave his employ to join in work with their family business rather than earn wages elsewhere only to have them taxed exorbitantly. In this situation, it turns out to their advantage. I am grateful that they have a business on which to concentrate their combined work effort rather than continue to be inordinately taxed while working for a company owned by someone else and see little return for that effort.

*Fourteen*

# NATIONALIZATION

And did the countenance Divine,
Shine forth upon our clouded hills?
And was Jerusalem builded here,
Among these dark Satanic Mills?

Jerusalem (And did those feet in ancient time)

--William Blake 1804

Nationalization gives the government overriding control of important services and transfers private assets of these services to public assets under the control of the state. In this transfer process, there is extraordinarily little if any room for religious values, and certainly not for dissension from traditional faith-based ideals. Aneurin Bevan, as the founder of the NHS, was the one who called for nationalization after WWII. He particularly rallied for the nationalization of the coal industry. The idea was that nationalization would accomplish three important goals for the socialist state 1) dispossess the large capitalist holdings, 2)divert the profits from private use to the public purse, and 3) ensure that the nationalized sector is in service of the public good instead of private profits.[55]

Upon close examination, there should have been clear indications of the dangers of the Nationalist Socialist German Workers' Party referred to as the Nazi Party of Germany from the early twentieth-century tragedy. Yet few modern socialists realize that the socialist state of Nazi Germany was a prime example of a destructive economic system based solely on government ownership of the means of production as dictated by the totalitarian ruler Adolf Hitler who required complete and unchallenged subservience to the state. It is ludicrous to refer to Nazi Germany as a capitalist system since most industries and businesses only appeared to be private enterprises. The means of production existed entirely in name as the *de facto* Nazi German government that wielded all the essential powers of ownership. The government made all decisions relating to the production of which included quantity, distribution, method, and pricing. There were even strict designations of wages, dividends, and income distribution to the in name only "private owners". For the Nazis, the private good was subservient to the common good. The *State* was the supreme authority and all that the individual considered to be property was indeed owned by the *State*.

An interesting study would be a case analysis of European political and economic systems and their functions after the Second World War. Exactly what happened to the major economies during the years after WWII when I was born? What ensuing political ideologies were introduced and what were the long-term effects? Nationalization of the United Kingdom's major services and austerity measures were the answers to major problems for the people and for the economy at the time. However, nationalism as the permanent solution turned into a case of the cure becoming worse than the disease.

In 1945, when Clement Atlee, who represented the Labour Party, defeated Winston Churchill as Prime Minister of England, his platform was based on nationalization. The election was shortly after World War II, not long before I was born. Resources were scarce, and jobs were even scarcer. Food rationing was still in practice since supplies had been marked and designated for the war effort. Nationalization designates the state as overseer of the means of production and distribution while capitalization encourages individuals to create their own business ventures and profit from the earnings. Nationalization also requires that any profits made will be used to the advantage of the country or the greater group of recipients instead of the smaller number of individuals benefiting from the company profits. It is important to note that nationalization can occur with or without compensation to the original owners.

The process of nationalization would **not** turn out to be a smooth transition in the UK. In the beginning, there were more problems than anticipated. The were problems of inefficiency that began to plague Industry along with dwindling profits. Without competition to motivate workers to perform better on the job, the overall job quality vigorously declined. Consequently, sales dropped considerably. There were, however, some notable improvements for workers. Coal miners received paid vacations and sick leave. Workplace safety began to be addressed. However, these improvements would eventually turn out to be realized at a remarkably high cost.

The newly formed government nationalized certain necessary public services such as transportation (bus and train), the steel industry, the postal services, the mining industry, the oil industry, and the gas and electric industry. The unions became extremely powerful and predominant to the extent that an increasing number of strikes among workers became commonplace. Instead of interviewing politicians, the press turned its attention to the union leaders who controlled the strikes, which then influenced the economy of the country. That is what awaits America regardless of the seemingly good intentions of the *fair-minded* politicians.

One of the more passionately, progressive Democratic Party candidates for the 2020 presidential election in the United States was a Senator from Massachusetts, Elizabeth Warren also, a former teacher and law professor. She founded her campaign on the premise that she had a *plan for everything*. But her *plans* were referred to as *nonstarters* and were deemed inadequate to those outside of academia. They were relevant only to those whose world revolves around the theoretical ideal instead of day-to-day, practical reality.

The stark memories showed the reality of the constant failings in the United Kingdom's Labour government attempts when running the nationalized businesses like the steel, coal, and railway industries. These memories contributed to a dismal outlook for a country that had once done incredibly well on the world's economic stage. I wondered if any of the passionate American voices in favor of a socialistic government had ever really experienced or even seen the despair and long-lasting malaise that comes from a labor government out of control. The folks that wanted to replace a free market economy like the one that the United States enjoyed, were inexperienced at what it means to live in socialistic circumstances.

I remember an experience that I had when taking a train to London from my hometown, Warrington. The ticket collector gave me the wrong ticket, so I needed to change it. The man adamantly refused to accommodate me and decided at that moment to walk away from the line and take his lunch. I was left without recourse while the ticket collector took care of himself. The customer was never right, while the worker's rights were always more important than the customer. People and, of course, employers were terrified of organized union workers. When I worked as an apprentice engineer, there was even a union leader over the apprentices. This is the fellow who enjoyed his influential power by calling a strike at least once a month for reasons as insignificant as late toast arriving for the breakfast break. This kind of thinking dominated the workforce. Productivity and eventually, goods and services were of lesser quality. The products were not able to compete with products from more stable world economies that were not severely restricted by burdensome taxation and labor restraints. Government fails when its intervention in the economy causes an incompetent appropriation of vital resources. Certain labor market restrictions that might include limiting work weeks and increasing minimum wages could ultimately result in problems with adjustability that could prevent companies from addressing increases in demand as well as producing unemployment. All of these kinds of problems began to cause trouble for the Labour governments of the United Kingdom.

My homeland in the northwest of England and the entire United Kingdom sadly began to resemble a playbook of austerity government measures influenced by restrictions on personal choices in the lives of her native sons and their families. Every human being is born with incredible, creative potential, regardless of his culture, color or creed. It is, however, up to the creature to find, nurture, develop, and use that potential or choose to allow that potential to be wasted, squandered, misused, destroyed, or repressed. Mankind was directed to "be fruitful and multiply" in the Garden of Eden by a creator who carefully created him in His image. He even tells us in Psalms 138: 6-8 NKJV that we can count on his help when we are in the middle of trouble (when we seek Him and depend on

Him); that He regards the lowly (humble); that He takes note of the proud, and that He will indeed perfect, that which concerns us, not forsaking us because of His everlasting mercy.

We realize through following God's teachings revealed in his word, that creative potential does not develop by repression nor does ability, nor does genius of any kind flourish in the context of human restriction. We can only know truth from a relationship with the God who is and who instructed us through Jesus to follow Him and to *"go and make disciples of all the nations."* (Matthew 28:19 NIV)

*Fifteen*

# EDUCATION

Don't know much about history
Don't know much biology
Don't know much about a science book
Don't know much about the French I took
But I do know that I love you
And I know that if you love me, too
What a wonderful world this would be.

Wonderful World

--Sam Cooke 1959

In the United Kingdom of the post-war years, education systems were inefficient at instruction because they did not teach but rather indoctrinated people by directing them to know and accept their birth status in the social hierarchy. I was one of forty students in my classrooms, and there were ten other boys named David in the same classroom in 1961. There was never more than one teacher available for forty children, and discipline was strict. There were consequences for those who misbehaved.

Until the social turbulence and cultural revolution of the sixties, it was the habit to preserve the status quo. The English educational institution available to the lower classes found its core in a socialistic system that looked for ways to eliminate competition among students in order to continually provide a solid, working class. During my children's school

113

days, as the socialistic government began to control various aspects of life in the UK, I recall the change from extending opportunities for higher levels of education for the more deserving students to an all-inclusive and comprehensive school system. At first glance, this seemed to be a fair and equitable designation of opportunity. As a matter of fact, comprehensive schools found mainly in the United Kingdom and based on a school program for secondary level children, no longer selected participants according to academic achievement or aptitude. This change put everyone on the same level and eliminated the concept of superior performers that were recognized according to their ability and potential. Instead of separating the students with the most potential and allowing them to progress according to their own ability and work ethic, there was a leveling of all groups thus contributing to a "dumbing-down" of students in general in the educational mainstream to fit the flawed system. When it was time to make distinctions concerning student performance, a series of tests and exams called the *eleven-plus*, or the *transfer test* was administered to all students. Their future secondary schooling was thus determined. If you didn't pass the exams given at age eleven, you could only go to the secondary modern school that provided for students who supposedly could not handle the superior programs of the grammar school with higher quality and levels of education. There was not much coaching or counseling so that students could understand or even prepare themselves for what to expect. I did not take school very seriously in those days and was interested in having fun along with my mates. I missed passing the exams by just a few points and was glad to have the wretched test behind me. Yet, on reflection, I missed out on better education opportunities along with so many other students. School children in the United Kingdom would have to wait for Margaret Thatcher's conservative government that focused on improving the quality of education for all students in the UK.

School, especially higher education in the major industrialized cities, was not seen as pertinent in my community during my early years since there were many skilled labor jobs available at the time in Warrington. We had nothing like homecoming weekend with football games or high school proms that linger in our memories throughout adulthood and help us to cherish fond recollections of the part that school played in our coming of age activities. One of my favorite movies about this American phenomenon is *Grease*. That inevitable happy American ending for Sandy and Danny played by Olivia Newton-John and John Travolta in high school was fondly observed in the UK, but never experienced. The thinking for my friends and me was more along the lines of living for today. *Why worry about meaningless facts and figures in school when it was easy to make a living in all the government established if not subsidized places provided by the state?* It is difficult to imagine that the American education system will improve from what it produces presently when a socialistic mindset and state will provide all the *free stuff.* Now, the questions from many American parents or at least the ones who are still concerned about their children's future seems to be more crucial. *Why should we, as parents, concern ourselves about quality education for our children, if the state will ultimately provide everything that they need? Or will it?* Clearly, we can no longer afford to ignore the necessity of quality education for all people if we are to have a healthy, functional society. Our inconsistencies and inadequacies will continue to haunt us and eventually cause increasingly disturbing and violent unrest.

Quality performance in the UK was no longer valued during the years of labour government initiatives and replaced with the attitude of mediocrity. Sufficiency was all that was needed. It was "just enough for government work." *Who needed an education if basic needs were to be provided by the government and paid for by the taxpayers?* The question here is what would inevitably become of bright performers who should have contributed to a superior academic pool and eventually evolve into a group of young people who would make significant contributions to the well-being of the nation in multiple areas?

I remember leaving school to work in a factory at the age of 15 as an apprentice engineer. My friends and I agreed that staying in school was of little value since there were plenty of jobs around and paychecks to be had at that moment. Never mind about the future since there was someone in the government to make certain that the workers would be *safe.* I was not discouraged in making this decision by anyone in my family, or by my peers. Even my teachers did not try to dissuade me in pursuing this kind of work since we were members of an industrial labor society in the northwest of England. I was not given a choice and certainly not another chance at the important exam that would determine the direction of my higher educational pursuit. Seeking higher education as preparation for the kind of lifestyle that would enable me to make decisions for myself, my children, and my future was not an option since there was only one chance to pass the exam. And of course, that also seemed determined by social class and eventually what kind of income I was destined to receive. The outcome of the eleven-plus examination worked to perpetuate the class divide that would claim the future dreams of generations of young students finishing their state-provided educations in working-class England.

I later left the apprenticeship after six years while ignoring the "friendly warnings" of fellow workers content to stay where they were without considering any other kind of work or lifestyle. They had grown comfortable with the "one size fits all" option. I soon began to realize that this kind of work would not lead to a future that I could enjoy, or that would match my desires and the pursuit of opportunities that matched my potential. During the transition to a socialistic government, the politicians seemingly lost control while the unions helped to take over.

In my life, I have seen that socialism may be attractive in theory but nearly always bad in practice. All aspects of any *one-size-fits-all* philosophy are inherently flawed. The inability of its designers to correctly discern human nature is the underlying problem. All human philosophies and man-made concepts are subject to failure because of destructive behaviors attributed to natural human tendencies. What about widespread abuses of any system? Are there adequate checks and balances in place? What is good in theory may be a grand failure in practice without a solid understanding of human nature and the record of the history of man is a good place to begin.

*Sixteen*

# AMERICA, TAKE NOTE

Wake up, Maggie, I think I got something to say to you
It is late September and I really should be back at school
I know I keep you amused, but I feel I'm being used
Oh, Maggie, I could not have tried any more

Maggie May

--Rod Stewart 1971

As a young man, I was very impressed with the generosity extended by the American people to nations in need throughout the world. This spirit of generosity has shown itself to be especially prevalent in countries where resources and availability of these resources was accessible to many. After World War II, when I was still quite a little lad, America financed the United Kingdom by extending generous aid as my country struggled to repair its financial course. America has headed the list of generous contributors on the world's stage for the larger part of the last century. Unfortunately, not all people in every culture will be fairly treated, offered access, or have the ability to utilize these resources. This sad fact is still a stain on the character record of humanity. But I continue to believe that if you pursue something with your whole heart and undivided focus, with God's help, you will be rewarded for persistent determination. Therefore, generosity should come naturally to those who are humble enough to realize that they are blessed.

Shortly after Barbara died, I was invited to play golf at the home of one of the other choir members. She and her husband were avid golfers, and I always enjoyed a good game. I had not purchased clubs since coming over from England, so my host and hostess supplied me with an excellent set of nearly new Ping clubs, a golf bag, and all the accessories, including the gloves to use for our game. At the end of the game, when I tried to give them back, my generous friends said, "Oh no! Those are yours to keep."

I am still excited when I think of the goal achieved by coming to live in America. I am even more excited as I reflect that my dreams and ideas have no limits even well into my *golden years*.

There is a proverb from Solomon's book of Proverbs 11:25 NKJV that says, "*The generous soul will be made rich, and he who waters will be watered*". These words remind me of a verdant garden that is well kept, well-watered, and well-tended, yielding abundant treasures for its fortunate recipients. My desire is that America should stay generous and well-watered to extend the same kind of generosity in the future.

The parable that Jesus told of the ten talents illustrates the importance of hard work and the proper investment of resources of all kinds. The story depicts a man of noble birth who, upon traveling to a distant country, gave ten of his servants a sum of money and a directive to put the money to work while he was away. When he returned, he found that only two men had acted according to his instructions and had profitably invested the money. A third servant had failed by fearfully, burying the talent until his return. The man rewarded the servant who diligently invested the money. The master took the money away from the fearful investor and awarded it to the most profitable investor who had shown courage, faith, and ingenuity. At the end of this story, Jesus replied, "*I tell to you that to everyone who has* (faith, courage, and persistence), *more* (faith, courage, persistence and even opportunity) *will be given, but as for the one who has nothing, even what they have will be taken away.*" Luke 19: 26 NIV (Interpretive notes from the author). We learn from this parable that Jesus came into the world not obsessed with money or materialism, but out of love and concern for people. He used the topic of money, which is very relatable to everyone, as an indication of our faith and of the responsibility to be good stewards. It is also our responsibility to use our talents and abilities to improve ourselves, our condition, and finally, to focus on the perpetuation of the Kingdom of

God. Self-improvement, wise choices, and faith in God will always result in an excellent profit.

The United States which has been the most successful capitalist economy the world has ever known, gives more financial support to struggling nations than any other civilization on earth. I was inspired by that generosity long before I arrived. No socialistic government has ever contributed even a fraction of what has been given by countries with free markets. That indicates that the abundance of resources and wealth are available only because of a capitalistic ideology directed by reasonable ethics and patrolled by its citizen benefactors. When this system falls into place under the authority of almighty God, it will produce a blessed people that can enjoy a prosperous lifestyle for all who are willing to pursue and protect it with persistent determination.

My good friend, Andy, reminds me that before I moved to America, I talked about Colonel Sanders (Kentucky Fried Chicken), who did not realize his dream until the age of seventy-two. Even though it came late, he would go on for another fifteen years and enjoy a successful venture and the realization of his dreams.

When I return to my homeland as a native son and walk through the town where I was born, I am now encouraged! I always wanted to see the best resources available to the people of the UK. When I visit my sons and their families today, I see the progress and even prosperity of the young moderns who work and live in the United Kingdom. I am thankful that Margaret Thatcher's vision linked with Ronald Reagan's ideas for economic growth provided stimulus and generated new programs. An example of the kind of stimulus that brought a change of mindset was a program that Margaret Thatcher introduced that allowed people to purchase government-owned property for extremely low prices. The rental council houses that they had lived in for years now became affordable. This opportunity encouraged them to improve their living conditions and led to thriving communities that reflected the pride of ownership. This extended program supplied housing opportunities for all citizens. The changes came slowly but are still taking place in most of the United Kingdom today.

Today, there is also the opportunity like never before to own a business, to own property, and to partake in higher education opportunities in the United Kingdom. The ability to pursue goals by going after a dream, to be in control of their futures, their choices and those of their offspring is now considered a commendable undertaking and an achievable goal. I notice the shiny, new vehicles driven throughout the country, along the motorways, and in the burgeoning cities. I remember well the desires that I had as a young boy to be a part of an economy so seemingly prosperous. I have been fortunate not only to live in America and experience what it means to enjoy the possibility of an advantageous lifestyle but also to see it become a realistic goal for my children and grandchildren who still reside in the United Kingdom. I am excited that my granddaughters are currently working in their chosen fields or pursuing university degrees. The little one that we chased through Walton Park trying to keep up with has recently finished law school. The boys are in various stages of their young lives and are also involved in pursuing their careers in sports and their educations in several different exciting fields. All of them are setting examples for the little ones and following the example of their parents who are now involved in directing their own businesses or working in management positions. I am proud to say their parents have done well in their careers and business enterprises. They are still working hard and are now enjoying the benefits of their labors. Expectations for the future are higher than I have ever seen in my lifetime. I see the tide turning, and I believe that my offspring will be able to continue to make good choices and enjoy the opportunities that are now available to them. These kinds of observations are quite rewarding, and I know that their mother would be so incredibly happy and proud of them all.

What is alarming to me is that the reality of a welfare state and its ideologies, for example, government care "from the cradle to the grave" for all, that pervaded post-war England is beginning to blow like a dark cloud drifting over the United States of America. We are beginning to see many willing supporters of welfare state mentality among young people who represent the future here in the United States and who think they are responding to calls for what they believe is progress. Although there will always be a need for improvements in the manner that we as human beings treat each other, we must be careful to examine what is being sold and packaged as progress. Questionable, socialistic ideologists with a lack of clear understanding of both human nature and economic reality are leading some to buy into what I foresee as a dangerous and potentially unstable future for themselves and America. What the socialist theorists are failing to reveal is that these changes to the American political and economic landscape will produce problems for them and for their children that may take them to the brink of unforeseen, long term, and devastating consequences. I lived through the dark days of multiple economic and sociological problems and know that the often-unseen impact will be a part of the landscape for years to come. That is exactly what happened in Great Britain until Margaret Thatcher took the reins. Recovery from bad government programs takes years and usually causes more harm than good.

*Seventeen*

# WHAT IS THE ANSWER?

When I am down, and, oh, my soul, so weary
When troubles come, and my heart burdened be
Then, I am still and wait here in the silence
Until you come and sit awhile with me

You raised me up so I can stand on mountains
You raise me up to walk on stormy seas
I am strong when I am on your shoulders
You raise me up to more than I can be

You Raise Me Up

--Josh Groban 2003

There is a lack of wisdom and unclear direction being packaged under the label of progress and then being sold to the American people as a desirable solution to social and economic problems that do not seem to be improving. There are endless questions about the exact nature of what they are proposing and supporting. *How much it will cost? Who will be required to pay? Who will watch over ethical decisions? Who will be held accountable? What will America become as she begins to fall behind rather than lead a volatile, world market?* Cal Thomas refers to the "free stuff" syndrome as an addictive notion resulting from several generations of people who, except for members of the military, have little or no idea of what it means to sacrifice for their country. Many of them have "bought into the idea that the rich people and big corporations are evil because they have stolen money from others, especially the poor."[56] What may be the most alarming prospects concern the proposed price tags, the tax increases, and the financial demands on unsuspecting and unwilling citizen victims who will be required to pay. The price tags are almost inconceivable and beyond the capacity of reason. These funds that will certainly be impossible to obtain, will still fall ridiculously short of the goal needed to sustain the proposed programs. It would have been like me and my mates at the Burtonwood airbase showing up to buy one of the world's most expensive fighter jets, the F-35C Joint Strike Fighter priced today at 120 million American dollars with the few coins we had collected returning used soda bottles.

When we examine countries like Venezuela, a supposedly shining example of a healthy socialistic state, we clearly understand the potential realities. The Venezuelan economy, which was once the most prosperous in South America, is now a dismal failure and a disappointing reality.

When I owned a small marketing business in the mid-nineties, a business associate asked me to represent him on a project in the Czech Republic shortly after the Berlin Wall came down. The Czech government, in partnership with the British Consulate, sponsored a group of businessmen to assist in promoting, advising, and enhancing new business practices. Upon arrival, it was starkly evident that the people of the Czech Republic had endured years of crippling poverty brought on by poor government management and had been drained of all resources. Prague, which had once been a beautiful and historical city, looked like it had never recovered from the devastations of WWII. We were shown around the city of Prague and its outskirts. The once regal buildings were blackened from soot and smoke that still continued in the nineties to pour into the skies out of rundown factories. There were more working prostitutes on the streets at night than there were people. The city displayed a hopeless and forbidding oppression. The group, with which I had traveled from the UK, consisted of business representatives who were to meet and advise local entrepreneurs. These prospective business owners needed ideas and advice for new enterprises and were exploring possibilities for potential partnerships. It was obvious that the Czechs were a people group hungry for stimulation and change from extreme leftist government policies. It was as if they were crying out for help. The city was at the edge of dereliction in the nineties and dangerously tottering on the precipice of the point of no return. During the latter part of the decade, free markets helped re-establish the once beautiful city back to a flourishing example of a modern European capital.

On closer examination, we see that there are no examples of successful socialistic economies. Countries like China, Denmark, Sweden, and France that socialist politicians regard as good examples of socialist states are various forms of free-market economies. **"Only a free-market capitalist economy can produce the wealth necessary to sustain all of the supposedly 'free stuff' (proposed by recent socialist political ideologists who claim) that Europeans enjoy."**[57] This *free stuff* requires an extremely large amount of tax revenue, generating enough wealth to cover the costs of the government *giveaways.*

I remember as a young boy having studied in school about the separation of Germany into two different countries after World War II and the construction of the Berlin Wall in 1961. East and West Germany were two separate countries in one space. The Soviet Union controlled East Germany and the Allied Forces controlled West Germany. In time, East Germany was given its independence. Eventually, East Germany under communist and socialist rule became unprofitable and unsustainable until the outstanding imperative of the American President Ronald Reagan in 1987, "Mr. Gorbachev, tear down this wall!"

Post-war England's welfare state provisions and Labour government regimes were leading the country to a dangerous decline. Margaret Thatcher's Conservative government helped the entrepreneur by encouraging opportunities for individual business start-ups and growing concerns, which in turn produced a strong economy. Most importantly, good-paying jobs became available to those who had lost employment during the years of socialistic Labour governments. It turns out that a free market economy was much more beneficial to the people of the United Kingdom.

> *Yet this I call to mind*
> *And therefore, I have hope.*
> *Because of the Lord's great love, we are not consumed,*
> *for His compassions never fail*

*They are new every morning*
*Great is your faithfulness.*
*I say to myself, "The Lord is my portion.*
*Therefore, I will wait for Him."*
*The Lord is good to those whose hope is in Him*
*To the one who seeks Him.*

Lamentations 3: 21-26 NIV

A Christ-centered worldview is one that holds to the teaching of "in Him, all things hold together." If he, Jesus Christ is indeed the cornerstone around which the building derives its strength, then all ideas must originate from him for the benefit of those for whom he lived and died. *"For God so loved the world that He gave His only begotten Son, that whoever believes in Him should not perish but have everlasting life."* (John 3:16 NKJV) But this same Jesus spoke of the stone which the builders rejected.

Not all will hold a Christ-centered worldview. The ideology of Karl Marx and Friedrich Engels' *Manifesto* claimed that the foundation of all history and social conflict is formed in the battle of class struggle, which is an ideology that vehemently pursued the abolition of private property and by association the annulment of private opinion. Their ideas most clearly denied the existence of a supreme creator to whom we should look for guidance on how we relate to each other. We do not have to go much further to see the fundamental differences between a Christ-centered worldview to a state-centered or in reality a self-centered/self-managed one.

Socialism focuses its program on the well-being of the state, which becomes the ultimate authority. This idea is opposed to the concept of the dominion of a supreme entity. There is no room for God in socialism, allowing only for the ideal of cooperation among its followers. Socialists hold to the belief that once capitalism and competition are extinguished, people will naturally want to cooperate. God is considered an unwelcome intruder (even though man is created in his image, and therefore no one knows us better than him). God's existence is explained away as "the opium of the people" by the disciples of Karl Marx.

Vladimir Lenin declared his attitude of the workers' party toward religion in a paper of the same title in May 1909. It is strongly implied in this paper that "it is the absolute duty of Social-Democrats to make a public statement of their attitude towards religion." The paper continues to describe Social-Democracy as having its entire world-outlook on scientific socialism, i.e., Marxism. The author, Lenin, explains that the basis of Marxism, as defined by Marx and Engels, is *dialectical materialism*,[58] which is, in fact, the same eighteenth-century materialism of France and Germany. What is most telling is that materialism, spoken of in this written work is, in truth, atheistic and positively hostile to religion. Lenin categorically declares that Marxism, the foundation for all socialistic thought is indeed materialism.[59]

The teachings of Jesus Christ have sometimes been taken hostage and wrangled to fit the ideologies of socialism and even its *religiophobic* close relation, communism. There are descriptions in the book of the Acts of the Apostles that record the early church teaching that "And God's grace was so powerfully at work among them that there were no needy persons among them."(see Acts 4:33-34 NIV) Yet these so-called Christian socialists conveniently leave out an important point; that those who believed (in Jesus, the Christ) were of one heart and soul giving testimony to the resurrection of the Lord Jesus. They also conveniently fail to acknowledge and communicate that to Him, all things belong, and in Him, all things hold together. In reality, Christ is not the philosophic center of these convenient socialist interpretations. But these examples from the early church writings have been conveniently twisted to convince less studied individuals that all things (material and physical) should be for the benefit of the group. How often have we seen this kind of corrupt message manifested in dangerous and deadly cult environments throughout modern history? How many more must we endure?

It is certain that no ideology, belief system, political party, economic theory, nor any philosophy of man will stand the test of time nor will it ever be able to address the pressing problems and deep needs of the hearts of all human beings. Ironically, these answers can never come from man alone even though we have been trying on our own for thousands of years without success.

All have sinned and come short of the glory of God. To sin is not merely an errant judgment or an act of rebellious disobedience. It is much more sinister in that it begins with an **errant heart and a rebellious and prideful spirit**, and that is exactly how we come into this world. Self is very much our center; our home base and we spend the rest of our lives seeking to manipulate the world around us into accommodating our errant inadequacy even at the cost of the well-being of others. We can twist all good ideas and the unmatched beauty that God intends this world to reveal into something selfish, horrible, and evil that can become devastating for all concerned. Where will it take us? Indeed, what IS going on?

There is only one answer for the hurt, pain, and destruction that we bring to a world originally created to be a refuge and safe harbor for our fragile humanity. Two thousand years ago, God came in the flesh to show us a different path. The creator of life himself miraculously came to teach us how to navigate the pathway of life. He did so with unfathomable love and unbelievable self-sacrifice in bearing the cost of connecting unholy and sinful human nature to a holy, omniscient, omnipresent, and omnipotent God. This Holy God initiated the process himself in sending, by way of that unfathomable love, the ultimate sacrifice of his only begotten son so that our sinful nature could be reconciled to this amazing Holy God. His only request is that we acknowledge our sinfulness, our inadequacy, and that we lay down our innate pride while turning our heart to him as we confess His dominion. We must make the choice individually to resign as the keeper of our own life and consequently acknowledge that only this Jesus, whom God sent, can be the sole keeper of mankind.

That is perhaps the most important lesson of my life and the source of the greatest wealth that I have ever known. Riches may also include but will never be limited to a bank account or reserves of wealth piled high even in some "secure" location. I have been blessed beyond measure to have grown up in a place of unmatched beauty like my homeland. I also understand with eyes wide open, the long-term consequences of living in a welfare state that was prone to making pathetic attempts at providing for a people who struggled to define right and wrong and to find a firm foundation through the second half of the twentieth century. True riches are measured by the knowledge of who I am, who I have been called to be, and what I have been called to do. All this knowledge comes from my relationship with God through Jesus Christ. As an additional incredible blessing, I have had the opportunity to live and prosper in America. This land of opportunity has been the realization of my lifelong goal. The riches of the knowledge of truth, freedom, and opportunity are incomparable.

Both the UK and the US, throughout decades and even centuries of aggressive leadership, have been painfully impacted by human error, greed, pride, racism, classicism, and various other grievous practices originating from our flawed human nature. Sadly, we are prone to continue making these errors in pursuit of rational and reasonable thinking. We cannot begin to fully understand the human experience either from an individual perspective, or corporately, or nationally, or internationally without God. He is the One who spoke the worlds into existence, without a creator who designed us and designed the universe according to his own inestimably perfect plan. We must seek him, Jesus, who provides us with access to the only living God. For Jesus is he who has risen, just as he said he would, far above the din and the clamor, far above the cry for help or shelter in the storm. Jesus enables us to pursue life to its richest and fullest form for all of eternity. We must seek the Saviour who lives, not the right philosophy that can only make a feeble and disappointing attempt at filling our hearts and our existence with meaning and purpose.

As a result of my life and experiences from post-war Great Britain through to the Great Britain that I see on the road to maintaining a healthy and strong economy, I am thoroughly convinced that the ideology of those who want the lure and promises of what they believe to be an equal society based on the provision by the state from the "cradle to the grave" will fail in America just as it has failed in every government system that has been unwise enough to give it a try even for a short period. I also know that doing nothing and saying nothing when wrong manifests itself can be more deadly than being on the unpopular side of the argument. **Wrong is still wrong even if everyone is doing it and right is still right even when no one is doing it**. The welfare state policies have been unsuccessful even seriously destructive in the United Kingdom and will probably if attempted in the United States result in long-term devastation such as never before experienced by the American people. The state will never replace freedom for any people to pursue their own dreams, regardless of where they call home. The precious promises of God, the strength of a nation and those certain unalienable rights belong to and rely upon individual freedom from restriction. They are always best appreciated from the perspective of liberty.

What exactly is liberty? Dictionary.com calls it *freedom from arbitrary or despotic government control; freedom from external or foreign rule; independence; freedom from control, interference, obligation, restriction, hampering conditions, etc.; power or right of doing, thinking, speaking, etc.*

*according to choice.* I personally am particularly fond of the last explanation although we understand that there is also freedom from physical restraint.

Capitalism as an ideology most closely resembles the freedom that Thomas Paine wrote about in his famous pamphlet "Common Sense" in 1776 while socialism more closely represents restrictive government control. The author admonishes writers not to confound society with government because the former is a result of our wants and the latter is produced by wickedness "negatively by restraining our vices…"

*"We still feel the greedy hand of government thrusting itself into every corner and crevice of industry and grasping at the spoil of the multitude. Invention is continually exercised to furnish new pretenses for revenue and taxation. It watches prosperity as its prey and permits none to escape without a tribute."*[60] Obviously, Thomas Paine was making reference to my ancestors on the shores of my homeland as they attempted to maintain a dominating hand of control over the rebellious cluster of colonies that strove for independence from tyranny in the late eighteenth century. I am now watching in stunned amazement as many American voices are calling for a return to the strong hand of government control against which they originally fought so valiantly while singing, *"Oh say can you see by the dawn's early light, what so proudly we hail at the twilights last gleaming?"*

Jesus came to set at liberty those who are held captive from wrong thinking, wrong ideas, wrong habits, those who are victims of prison-like limitations, and those suffering from defeated mindsets. He alone can set us free from reliance on those who are opposed to liberty in any form. He came to set us free from captors whose despotic tyranny is abusive and directed towards the weak and ignorant, to set us free from evil and oppressive weights that have been leveled through the ages upon many who have seen their dreams destroyed. This same tyrant throughout history has pursued those without hope, those who have faced dark futures, those who have shed tears of frustration, and those who are already suffering from fear of failure and hopelessness. But we need only to look toward Him, who came to set the captives free.

We are all much too familiar with what captivity looks and feels like after having endured weeks of separated isolation and "social distancing" to stop the spread of another kind of tyrannical force. We should hope to only endure this kind of physical captivity once in our lives even though having time for quiet reflection, life evaluation and pursuit of what we value most without constant distractions of the hustle and bustle of western living was hopefully a silver lining in the cloud of inconvenience. We certainly do not want to be confined because of our beliefs or by intruding government forces "*from the cradle to the grave*".

Prince Harry Mountbatten-Windsor has given us a contemporary illustration after having to watch his beloved mother, as well as his beautiful wife, suffer a similar torment at the hands of the British tabloids. They went to great lengths to design, fabricate and exaggerate stories of the Sussex couple for the sole purpose of improving circulation and monetary gain. Meghan Markle, now known as Meghan Mountbatten-Windsor, reminded us in a poignant interview that "it was not enough to just survive our life experiences." She said that we need to thrive within them. It was not long after those words that Harry decided to usher his young family to safety, referring to the pressure of this kind of unrelenting, destructive attention as "dark and powerful forces". The desire to manipulate other human beings, rendering them victims and targets of sinister enterprises and for selfish and destructive financial gain or domination over others, is a stark illustration of the worse kind of human exploitation. This desire has found breeding ground within all the philosophies of the human experience. Sadly, the history of mankind has given us too many examples. Therefore, we need to be free to pursue relationship with the One who created and loved us enough to save us.

We need to be set free even from ourselves regardless of our background and belief. ML King reminded Americans in the sixties of the importance of freedom. Government restrictions and choices made only by the leaders of that government, in turn, severely restrict and even cripple opportunity. America should never forget the government by the people, of the people and for the people. Somewhere underneath the foundation of those unforgettable words is the cry for freedom. Freedom can only ring without government restrictions and limitations.

It has been my personal experience that free-market ideologies that are capitalistic in practice and perspective have enabled me to pursue my goals and to anticipate bright futures for my children and grandchildren.

The riches I now enjoy are beautifully packaged and carefully encompassed in unlimited opportunities and numerous possibilities up to any age. I am thankful beyond measure for what God has made available to me and enabled me to achieve. I am even thankful to be able to recognize it. I am thankful for the opportunity to gaze on those purple mountain majesties, on both of those shining coastal seas and to anticipate the amazing future here and on through to eternity. I am thankful for vision and the ability to look beyond any present circumstances or limitations to the best that is undoubtedly yet to come. I am convinced that my dad, Jack, would have been delighted.

The most precious resource is full of the untold richness that can only come from a relationship with the One who came to give us life and that abundantly. In Jesus Christ and Him alone, we can understand what it means to be a child of God with all the benefits and blessings that accompany sonship. The list is unlimited, the favor abundant, the mercies enduring throughout eternity, the assurance blessed, the provision guaranteed, the protection granted. As we seek first His kingdom, all these things will be added to our lives.

Some things do not change. Humans of all cultures will continue to need reasonable shelter, food, and clothing. Our children will need instruction and education. They will also need to attain solid values and pursue ethical behavior. They will need to acquire morality. If we are to co-exist and our children are to procreate, we will all need to take responsibility for our own choices and our well-being. We will need to work and to be fairly compensated for that work for in all labour there is profit while idle chatter will always lead to poverty as Solomon warned. We will always need fairness and equity in our life choices, realizing that there will always be consequences to our behavior and for our choices. We will need to respect and trust each other to a reasonable extent in order to live side by side with a limited number of valuable resources. But those limitations must come from God as we seek and obey His will. We will need freedom, self-expression, protection, diversity, intelligence, access to information, health services, hope, direction, and purpose. We will most definitely need persistence, determination, and encouragement, even if it only comes from our building ourselves up on our own most holy faith. Perhaps most importantly, we will need truth, value, self-esteem, self-respect, equality, dignity, and love, all coming directly from a strong tie with God as Father.

Theoretical ideas do not work well when they overlook the basic need all humans have, which is the opportunity to rise to their highest potential. Any intention that short circuits creativity or undermines opportunity as essential elements by offering *free handouts* is doomed to fail. These *handouts* represent poor substitutes for hard-earned accomplishment, for mountains scaled, for rivers and oceans crossed, for grueling battles won, or for all outstanding, unreachable goals attained. *Free handouts* cannot and will not endure the annals of history of which we find ourselves an inescapable part.

In those poignant words of the prophet Jeremiah, God tells His people, "*I know the plans I have for you...plans to prosper you and not to harm you, plans to give you hope and a future. Then you will call on **me** and come and pray to **me**, and I will listen to you. You will seek **me** and find **me** when you seek **me** with all your heart. I will be found by you...*" Jeremiah 29:11-14 NIV (emphasis by the author)

What an astounding promise and an incredible reminder that God desires that those who belong to Him will do well and have hope for all eternity!

In the final analysis, we need Jesus far more than politics. He said that no man could come to the Father, who is God except by Him. Jesus is constant, eternal, the Way, the Truth, and the Life. Without Him, we are perpetually and eternally lost, following a lie and without true life.

Politics and the systems of this world will change with the wind. They will never succeed in saving anyone or anything. Man's ideas and the continual exchanging of power between one influential group and leader and the next one have always failed to provide for man's needs. They always will.

There is only one solution. You must give your life to Jesus Christ with full acknowledgment that this life is impossible without Him and that you need His saving grace. If we are ever to understand fully what this life is about, we need His guidance.

On my journey, I have learned that the game of life is played on the field, not on the sidelines in the safety zone. We must launch out into the deep, full, abundant life that only God has for us. We should be incredibly careful not to let anyone else define us or place limitations on who we are or what we are called to be through politics and group manipulation tactics.

We cannot find him as a part of a group and certainly not merely through cooperation with a group. We can learn and grow from being a part of a fellowship with other believers, but first, he calls to us as individuals, and one must respond with his/her own whole heart. One must stand up for who God created him or her to be and then do what God requires to serve Him. There is no greater joy than knowing that you are His. In Him, we have hope. In Him, we live and move and have our being.

I understand that I could never exceed the blessing of the eternal riches of knowing a God who loves me unconditionally. God is the one with whom I have a privileged relationship not based on myself nor my selfish accomplishments but based on the price that Jesus paid to extend to me as a believer, access to a holy God whom I call Father. I am so much more than I could have ever been, and more than I could ever be without him. His riches, the riches of God, will always exceed even the greatest benefits of any system that we could ever imagine without Him.

### All Things Made New

*And I heard a loud voice from heaven saying, "Behold, the tabernacle of God is with men, and He will dwell with them, and they shall be His people. God Himself will be with them and be their God. And God will wipe away every tear from their eyes; there shall be no more death, nor sorrow, nor crying. There shall be no more pain, for the former things have passed away."*

*Then He who sat on the throne said, "Behold, I make all things new." And He said to me, "Write, for these words are true and faithful."*

*And He said to me, "It is done! I am the Alpha and the Omega, the Beginning and the End. I will give of the fountain of the water of life freely to him who thirsts. He who overcomes shall inherit all things, and I will be his God and he shall be My son.* **Revelation 21: 3-7 NKJV**

Saint James's Park in London

Chester Cathedral near Warrington

Jack, David and sons 1979

David's family in Warrington on his 70th Birthday 2019

David and Friends celebrate him

Lynette at Starrs Mill in Fayette

Beach at Destin, Florida

Lighthouse at Hilton Head Island, South Carolina

# NOTES

1   Matt Chorley and Jason Groves, "The Letter that will haunt Labour on the eve of yet more cuts", accessed April 1, 2020, www.dailymail.co.uk/news.

2   Christopher Hope and Paul Stokes, "Warrington is ranked at the bottom of Government-backed quality of life survey", *The Telegraph*, December 9, 2009.

3   "Five Things You Should Know About Warrington," *Cheshire Life*, March 13, 2014 accessed April 24, 2020.

4   Aldon Ferguson, "RAF Burtonwood Fifty Years In Photographs," *Burtonwood Airfield Publications*, (Reading:1986), p. 9.

5   Aria Bendix, "The US was once a leader for healthcare and education – now it ranks 27th in the world," *businessinsider.com*, accessed April 20, 2020.

6   Marvin Perry, Myrna Chase, Margaret Jacob, James R. Jacob, *Western Civilization: Ideas, Politics and Society- From 1600*, Volume 2, Ninth Edition, (Boston: Houghton Mifflin Harcourt Publishing, 2009), p. 540.

7   Keith Taylor, *Henri de Saint Simon, 1760-1825: Selected Writings on Science, Industry and Social Organization*. (New York, USA: Holmes and Meir Publishers, Inc, 1975). Pp. 158-161.

8   Alan Ryan, *On Politics: A History of Political Thought: From Herodotus to the Present*, Book II. (New York: Liverhigh Publishing, 2012), Pp. 647-651.

9   Eugene Lee, "John Stuart Mill's On Liberty", *The Victorian Webb*, accessed April 14, 2020.

10  Kimberly Amadeo, "Socialism and its Characteristics, Pros, Cons, Examples and Types", *US Economy and News*, accessed March 16, 2020, https://www.thebalance.com/socialism-types-pros-cons-examples-3305592

11  Andy Puzder, "Capitalism vs Socialism," accessed April 25, 2020, www.prageru.com.

12  Steve Schifferes, "Britain's long road to the welfare state", *BBC News*, July 26, 2005.

13  Star Parker, *Uncle Sam's Plantation: How Big Government Enslaves America's Poor and What We Can do About It.* (Thomas Nelson, 2003, 2010), pp. 3-6.

14  JB Cachila, "3 Signs of a Poverty Mentality," *Christian Today*, December 7, 2016.

15    Derek Fraser, *The evolution of the British welfare state: a history of social policy since the Industrial Revolution*. (London: Palgrave McMillan, 2004), p. 233.

16    Gosta Esping-Andersen, *The Three Worlds of Welfare Capitalism*. (Princeton, New Jersey: Princeton University Press; Policy press), 1998

17    Paul Gregory and Paul Stuart, *The Global Economy and its Economic Systems*. (South-Western College Publishers, 2013), p.107.

18    Kimberly Amadeo, "Capitalism: Its Characteristics with Pros and Cons", *US Economy and News*, accessed March 2020 https://www.thebalance.com/capitalism-characteristics-examples-pros-cons-3305588,

19    C. Bradley Thompson, *Socialism vs Capitalism: which is the Moral System*. On Principle, Ashbrook Ashland University Publications, October 1993.

20    Brian Abel-Smith, "The Beveridge report: Its origins and outcomes." *International Social Security Review (1992) 45#1-2 pp. 5-16.*

21    Mckenna Moore, "Rep. Maxine Waters Tells Supporters to Harass Trump Cabinet Members," *Fortune*, June 25, 2018. Accessed April, 2020, https://fortune.com/2018/06/25/rep-maxine-waters-tells-supporters-to-harass-trump-cabinet-members/.

22    Martin Robinson, "So what if I'm on the dole?" Mother of ten children by FIVE fathers now wants 50 grandchildren to keep benefits rolling in", *MAIL.ONLINE*, accessed April, 2010, https://www.dailymail.co.uk/news/article-3087519.

23    Star Parker, "Why We Should Start Going Back to Work," www.creators.com accessed may 9, 2020, http://www.starparker.com/a/1378/why-we-should-start-going-back-to-work.

24    Thaddeus Williams, "Christian Millennials and the Lure of Socialism, Part One," *The Good Book Blog*, accessed May, 2020, https://www.biola.edu/blogs/good-book-blog/2016/christian-millennials-and-the-lure-of-socialism-part-two-how-biblical-concern-for-the-poor-can-turn-to-an-unbiblical-understanding-of-people.

25    John Campbell, *The Iron Lady: Margaret Thatcher from grocer's daughter to Prime Minister*. (London: The Penguin Group, 2009), p. 95.

26    Martin Gilbert, *Churchill: A Life*. (London: Rosetta Books, 2004). p. 92.

27    Jose harris, *William Beveridge: a biography*. (Clarendon Press, 1997), pp. 1, 323.

28    Neil Cooper, "Play tells the inspiring story of political couple Aneurin Bevan and Jennie Lee," *The Herald*, October 31, 2018.

29    Paul Kengor, "The Religious Left Just Doesn't Get It: Socialism Is Anti-Christian," *Crisis Magazine,* September 11,2019.

30    Jennie Neufield, "Alexandria Ocasio-Cortez is a Democratic Socialist of America," *Vox*, accessed May 2, 2020, https://www.vox.com/policy-and-politics/2018/6/27/17509604/alexandria-ocasio-cortez-democratic-socialist-of-america.

31  Ken Knight, "Lizard conspiracist David Icke Not Wanted in Berlin," *Made for Minds,* February 23, 2017, accessed May 4, 2020. https://www.dw.com/en/lizard-conspiracist-david-icke-not-wanted-in-berlin/a-37693384.

32  "Coronavirus: David Icke's Channel deleted By YouTube," *BBC News:Technology,* May 2, 2020, accessed May 4, 2020, https://www.bbc.com/news/technology-52517797.

33  "The Day David Icke Told Terry Wogan 'I'm the son of God,'" *The Telegraph,* accessed May 4, 2020. https://www.telegraph.co.uk/only-in-britain/david-icke-terry-wogan-interview/.

34  Charles Lehrman, "Alexandria Ocasio-Cortez's Green New Deal is Pretty Much All Fantasy land," *The Washington Free Beacon*, December 8, 2018.

35  Dennis Campbell, "NHS Suffering worst ever staff and cash crisis, figures show," *The Guardian*, September 11, 2018, accessed April, 2020, https://www.theguardian.com/society/2018/sep/11/nhs-suffering-worst-ever-staff-cash-crisis-figures-show.

36  Gov.UK accessed May 2020, https://www.gov.uk/income-tax-rates

37  Shaun Lintern, "50,000 patients in England now waiting over a year for treatment", *The Independent*, August 13, 2020.

38  "PA Media, Nursing shortages forcing NHS to rely on less qualified staff-report", *The Guardian*, November 27, 2019.

39  Denis Campbell, "NHS Suffering worst ever staff and cash crisis, figures show," *The Guardian,* September 11, 2018.

40  Denis Campbell, "NHS England losing staff in record numbers over long hours – study," *The Guardian,* Feb 16, 2019.

41  Ben Johnson, "Why the UK Suddenly is Suffering from a Physician Shortage," *Foundation for Economic Education.* June 1, 2019. accessed April, 2020, https://fee.org/articles/why-the-uk-suddenly-is-suffering-from-a-physician-shortage/.

42  "The NHS budget and how it has changed" *The Kings Fund* Newsletter, 05 September 2019 - Sources: Department of Health and Care annual report and accounts 2017/18 and 2018/19, Public Expenditure Statistical Analyses, July 2019, Spending round, September 2019 *Data are the Department of Health and Social Care total departmental expenditure limit (TDEL). Figures are in real terms at 2019/20, based on HM Treasury deflators from June2019.

43  Ben Johnson, "Why the UK Suddenly is Suffering from a Physician Shortage," June 1, 2019.

44  www.*Bupa.com, accessed* March 4, 2020.

45  Chris Smyth, The Times Whitehall Editor, October 31, 2019, accessed March, 2020, "https://www.thetimes.co.uk/edition/news/general-election-2019-plans-for-three-tv-debates-but-only-for-main-parties-b38s6x9sl.

46  Sam Blanchard, Senior Healthcare Reporter for Mailonline.com & David Wilcock, Whitehall Correspondent for Mailonline.com, December 2, 2019.

47  Eleanor Hayward, "Health Reporter," *The Daily Mail*, October 25, 2019.

48 Liam Thorpe, "Liverpool on the Brink of Collapse Due to Perfect Storm," *Liverpool Echo*, May 1. 2020.

49 Mark Andrews, "Misery Monday: Then was the winter of Our Discontent," The *Shropshire Star,* accessed April 25, 2020.
https://www.shropshirestar.com/resizer/KHIEXhO53I12f0RGIodOX B6W2aQ=/990x0/filters:quality(100)/arc-anglerfish-arc2-prod-shrop shirestar-mna.s3.amazonaws.com/public/ZVY6NUX6AVDQ3OTM QQR2TC3VAI.jpg

50 Mark Andrews, "Misery Monday," *The Shropshire Star,* accessed April 25, 2020 https://www.shropshirestar.com/news/politics/2019/01/26/misery-monday-then-was-the-winter-of-our-discontent/.

51 Helen Grady, "The English city that wanted to 'breakaway' from the UK," *The BBC News Magazine,* November 8, 2014.

52 Nick Sorrentino, "How the Beatles Dealt With a 98% Income Tax (That's right 98%)," *AC2 News,* accessed May 9, 2020, https://www.ac2news.com/2013/03/how-the-beatles-dealt-with-a-98-income-tax-thats-right-98/.

53 Nick Sorrentino, "How the Beatles Dealt With a 98% Income Tax," *AC2 News,* accessed May 9, 2020,

54 David Henderson, "Marginal Tax Rates: Singing *Taxman* to My Class," *EconLog,* accessed May 9, 2020. https://www.econlib.org/archives/2014/01/marginal tax ra 3.html.

55 Alec Nove, *The Economics of Feasible Socialism Revisited.* (London: HarperCollins 2005).

56 Cal Thomas, "Why Socialism Fails," *The Citizen, Opinion* March 20, 2019

57 Andy Pudzer, Capitalism vs. Socialism, accessed April 25, 2020, www.prageru.com.

58 Dialectical materialism is defined in the *Oxford Dictionary of English* as the Marxist theory (adopted as the official philosophy of the soviet communists) that political and historical events result from the conflict of social forces and are interpretable as a series of contradictions and their solutions. The conflict is seen as caused by material needs.

59 Vladimir Lenin, Public Domain Marxist Internet Archive, accessed April 14, 2020, https://www.marxists.org/archive/lenin/works/1905/dec/03.htm Materialism is defined here as a tendency to consider material possessions and physical comfort as more important than spiritual values. (*Oxford Dictionary of English*).

60 Thomas Paine, "Common Sense: Of the Origin and Design of Government In General, with concise Remarks On the English Constitution," accessed May 22, 2020, www.TheCapitol.Net.

# END MATTER PHOTOS

David in his office at home

Lynette